STALIN

MORE WILDSIDE CLASSICS

STALIN

by

MARTY BLOOMBERG

and

BUCKLEY BARRY BARRETT

WILDSIDE PRESS

STALIN

This edition published in 2006 by Wildside Press, LLC.
www.wildsidepress.com

CONTENTS

4

INTRODUCTION

Joseph Stalin was perhaps the most "successful" dictator in modern history and certainly one of the most important. Born of poor parents in Georgia, a backwater of the Russian Empire, Iosif Vissarionovich Dzhugashvili (his birth name) was not a likely candidate to become one of the most powerful dictators in history. Stalin's influence permeated almost every aspect of Soviet history for a quarter of a century, and "Stalinism" was still a ghost haunting Russia in 1993, as both researchers and political scientists tried to comprehend the disintegration of the Soviet Union.

This bibliography presents a select body of literature on Joseph Stalin and Stalinism. Entries are limited to books and translations in English. The intended audience is the non-specialist. Therefore, we have included only a limited number of books and intend them to present only an overview. The reader seeking in-depth coverage for a topic should refer to the bibliographies in many of the books cited in this bibliography and to specialized bibliographies on Soviet and Russian history.

Our guide is not intended to be all-inclusive. The authors have selected titles on the basis of one or more of the following criteria: 1) book reviews, 2) frequency of citations in other books and bibliographies, 3) reputation of the author, and 4) the authors' own reading and judgment. Wherever possible, several books on a topic have been cited, both to give the reader a choice as well as to represent differing points of view.

Books are arranged by subject, then alphabetically by author or editor, or by title if no author can be identified. Each entry includes basic bibliographic data, indicates if the book has a bibliography, and provides a brief descriptive and evaluative annotation. Mention of a bibliography can refer to a bibliography or to important bibliographic references or footnotes.

Work on this book was accomplished in the libraries of the California State University, San Bernardino, the University of California, Riverside, and the University of California, Los Angeles. Special thanks goes to Linda Evans for preparing the manuscript. Our appreciation also goes to Mike and Mary Burgess of Borgo Press for their invaluable editing.

—Marty Bloomberg and Buckley Barry Barrett
California State University, San Bernardino
June 30, 1993

CHRONOLOGY

1879 Iosif Vissarionovich Dzhugashvili born 21 Dec. (9 Dec. Old Style) at Gori, Russian Georgia.

1894 Enters a theological seminary at Tbilisi (Sept.)

1899 Dismissed from seminary.

1901 Elected to Tbilisi Social Democrat Committee.

1902 Arrested for first time after demonstration he organizes.

1903 Marries Ekaterina Svanidze, and is deported to Siberia.

1904 Son, Yakov, born. Escapes from Siberia and becomes a Bolshevik.

1905 Meets Lenin at a Bolshevik congress in Finland.

1906 Participates in bank robberies to increase party funds.

1907 Publishes "Anarchism or Socialism?" Goes to London for party congress. Ekaterina Dzhugashvili dies.

1908 During next three years is arrested, exiled, and re-exiled to Siberia. Adopts the revolutionary name Stalin.

1914 World War I begins.

1917 Tsar Nikolai II abdicates (March). Stalin returns to Petrograd. Bolsheviks oust the provisional government (Oct.); Stalin joins the new regime.

7

1918 Marries Nadezhda Allilueva. Russian civil war begins.

1919 Elected to Politburo and Orgburo.

1921 Son Vasilii born. Supervises occupation of Georgia.

1924 Lenin dies. Stalin begins formal attack on Trotsky.

1926 Birth of daughter, Svetlana. Zinoviev, Kamenev, Trotsky expelled from Politburo.

1929 First Five-Year Plan. Bukharin removed from Politburo. Collectivization begins.

1932 Introduces "socialist realism" for art. Nadezhda dies.

1936 Great purge begins (through 1938). Beria named head of secret police (1938).

1939 Secret treaty with Germany. Poland divided by Germany and Soviet Union. World War II begins.

1940 U.S.S.R. annexes the three Baltic states.

1941 Germany invades Soviet Union.

1943 Meets with Roosevelt and Churchill at Tehran.

1945 Hitler defeated. Stalin meets allied leaders at Yalta.

1948 Berlin blockade by U.S.S.R. and airlift by U.S. President Tito of Yugoslavia breaks with Stalin.

1949 U.S.S.R. tests its first nuclear bomb. Purge against Jews.

1950 Chinese-Soviet friendship treaty. Korean War begins.

1953 Death of Stalin (5 March); Beria executed.

1956 Khrushchev secretly denounces Stalin at party congress.

ABBREVIATIONS

C.P.S.U.: Communist Party of the Soviet Union
Cominform: Communist Information Bureau
Comintern: Communist International
KGB: Committee for State Security
NEP: New Economic Policy
N.K.V.D.: People's Commissariat for Internal Affairs
R.A.P.P.: Russian Association of Proletarian Writers

A.

BIOGRAPHIES, MEMOIRS, AND RELATED WORKS

BIOGRAPHIES AND MEMOIRS (PRE-1954)

A1. **Backer, George.** *The Deadly Parallel: Stalin and Ivan the Terrible.* New York: Random House, 1950, 240 p.

Some critics judged the parallel argument weak because of perceived cultural and political differences between the two rulers and the two eras, and many reviewers found Backer's wandering technique disconcerting. The author does reason with some strength, however, that the micro-controlled Stalinist historians praised Ivan enough to invite at least propagandistic personality comparisons.

A2. **Barbusse, Henri.** *Stalin: A New World Seen Through One Man.* New York: Macmillan, 1935, 315 p.

Reviewers described this work as propaganda for the Soviet system and a "work of hero worship" in its treatment of Stalin. For example, Stalin's role in the 1917 revolution is enlarged, while Trotsky's role—which was far greater—is practically eliminated. The author knew Stalin personally. The work is of interest both as propaganda and as an example of a developing cult literature, but must be approached cautiously as serious biography.

A3. **Basseches, Nikolaus.** *Stalin.* New York: E. P. Dutton, 1952, 384 p.

11

The author worked as a foreign correspondent in Moscow until 1937, and thus had first-hand experience with the Soviet leader. Critics generally felt that Basseches had produced a somewhat uncontrolled work but one with journalistic appeal. They also thought he had not broken past many of the Soviet myths and that this work did not compare with those produced by Deutscher, Fischer, Wolfe, or other, more scholarly writers. Basseches portrays Stalin as a man who succeeded because of his humble origins and who was sometimes bothered by conscience. Translated from the German original.

A4. **Bazhanov, Boris.** *Bazhanov and the Damnation of Stalin.* Athens: Ohio University Press, 1990, 285 p., bibliography.

A personal account of Stalin's rise to power between 1923-28. Bazhanov was briefly Stalin's assistant and secretary of the Politburo from 1923 to 1925 before defecting in 1928. While some good anecdotes about Lenin and Stalin are included, some caution is necessary on the part of the reader, since several scholars have claimed that Bazhanov exaggerated his role in the events he describes. The book was originally published in France in 1930 and expanded in 1979. This translation is based on the 1979 French edition, and includes an excellent introductory overview of the era.

A5. **Beriia [i.e., Beria], Lavrentii Pavlovich.** *On the History of the Bolshevik Organizations in Transcaucasia.* New York: International Publishers, 1991, 206 p.

This work is of interest primarily because of the role given to Stalin in pre-Revolution events in Transcaucasia. Written during the development of the "Stalin Cult," the work changes and exaggerates Stalin's role while rewriting history for political purposes. This history is of limited use as "real" history but valuable as an example of a "cult" revisionist history. Beria later became head of the

Soviet secret police, and was executed shortly after Stalin's death. Based on a speech delivered in 1935.

A6. **Bohlen, Charles E.** *Witness to History, 1929-1969.* New York: W. W. Norton & Co., 1973, 562 p.

The author served intermittently in the U.S. Embassy in Moscow from the time of its opening in 1934 until the late 1960s. His remembrances show an entertaining style and a keen—if not academic—perception. In trying to analyze Stalin, Bohlen gives us interesting diplomatic vignettes and comments, but admittedly struggles with a dilemma shared by other observers and researchers: the Soviet leader's warm and sometimes modest style with Western statesmen simply gave no hint whatsoever as to his monstrous and calculated inhumanity. Bohlen attributed Stalin's cruelty to a cold, Tartar-like persona.

A7. **Delbars, Yves.** *The Real Stalin.* London: George Allen & Unwin Ltd., 1953, 439 p., bibliography.

The author claims to have based this book on a decade of study and observation, and to have "carefully verified" the evidence and documents in creating a work of "strict objectivity"—Preface. These claims may sound naive or impossible for any biography of such a secretive and all-powerful dictator. Nevertheless, Delbars portrays Stalin's life as an ironic attempt to combine nationalism and communism. The result of the dictator's efforts is described not as practical Marxism, but as a highly regimented bureaucracy that controlled all capital and was protected by its political police and by a worried old man. The book was completed just prior to Stalin's 1953 death.

A8. **Deutscher, Isaac.** *Stalin: A Political Biography.* 2nd ed. New York: Oxford University Press, 1967, 661 p., bibliography.

Deutscher's text is considered a classic analysis of Stalin's political career, with the author's conclusions and facts holding up well in view of the materials now being released under glasnost. The author was expelled from the party in 1932 for political deviation, and writes from the perspective of the embittered émigré. Deutscher sees Stalin as the betrayer of the Revolution, one who deviated from its goals in order to acquire personal power. Originally published in 1949, the second edition added new materials on Stalin's last years.

A9. **Eastman, Max.** *Stalin's Russia and the Crisis in Socialism.* New York: W. W. Norton, 1940, 284 p.

Eastman blames Stalin for turning the Soviet Union too far away from the utopian path of true socialism. The author was known for, among other things, trying to view Marxist philosophy as more of a religious than political movement.

A10. **Fischer, Louis.** *Gandhi and Stalin: Two Signs at the World's Crossroads.* New York: Harper & Bros., 1947, 183 p.

Fischer asserts that the two figures of the title represent polar opposites in their political philosophies, and that we must resist the negativity of Stalinism. A fusion of individual and capitalistic democrary is exhorted along with a strong atomic defense. More of a polemic than a biography, although the powerful personna of Stalin has drawn many commentators and potential biographers past the normal boundaries of nonfiction to one extent or another.

A11. **Fischer, Louis.** *The Life and Death of Stalin.* New York: Harper & Bros., 1952, 272 p.

This biography is of interest now primarily as an example of a popular work of the 1950s. The author, who lived for years in Russia, offers some useful insights into Soviet life in the 1920s and 1930s. Also of interest is the author's psychological analysis of Stalin. Overall, a weak book which received mixed reviews when published.

A12. **Graham, Stephen.** *Stalin: An Impartial Study of the Life and Work of Joseph Stalin.* Port Washington, NY: Kennikat Press, 1970, 148 p., bibliography.

A reprint of a 1931 work that likened Stalin to a cunning tactician building upon the strong plans of Lenin. The author wrote that the first Five-Year Plan was succeeding and that the mechanization of agriculture was not likely to fail...all thanks to the wisdom, organizational talent, and motivational skills of Stalin. An early example of a somewhat optimistic view of the Soviet leader, although one should obviously remember that the massive purges of the later 1930s had not yet occurred, and that people may not yet have shown as much cynicism or skepticism about information coming out of the U.S.S.R.

A13. **Krivitsky, Walter G.** *In Stalin's Secret Service.* New York: Harper & Bros., 1939, 273 p.

An undocumented expose of Stalin's shift toward autocracy for its own sake. The author—whose name was fictionalized according to some reviewers—claims to have served as head of Soviet intelligence in Western Europe. Chapters cover such topics as early appeasement of Hitler, double-dealing against the Spanish loyalists, and "wet" removal of the generals. Portions of the book appeared in *The Saturday Evening Post*, and the work also appeared as *I Was Stalin's Agent*.

A14. **Levine, Isaac Don.** *Stalin.* New York: Cosmopolitan Book Corporation, 1931, 421 p., bibliography.

This work is of interest for several reasons. First, it is one of the earliest biographies of Stalin in English. Next, its leftist author's restrained criticism of Stalin may represent a precursor of future authors even more disillusioned with this dictator but not with the Soviet ideology.

Also noteworthy are the early psychological explanations of Stalin based on his years of flight and underground life and on the alleged cruelty of the Eurasian personality. Levine credits Stalin with transforming Russia into an industrial and economic power, while crediting Lenin for developing the foundation on which Stalin built. There is good material on conditions in Russia and on Stalin's political struggle as seen by a contemporary. A generous amount of material on the Trotsky-Stalin struggle is also included.

A15. *The Life of Stalin: A Symposium.* New York: Worker's Library Publishers, 1930, 96 p.

A typical work of propaganda written during the early phase of the Stalin Cult, the value of this work is as an example of early cult literature. The contributors—most of whom did not survive Stalin—include Manuilsky, Kaganovich, Voroshilov, Ordzhonikidze, and Yenukidze.

A16. **Ludwig, Emil.** *Stalin.* New York: G. P. Putnam's Sons, 1942, 248 p.

Generally excoriated at the time of its publication for its inaccuracies and lack of new insight, this title yet holds some interest. Ludwig was an early popular historian, and Russia shared the Allied burden in a "popular" war. Hence, the reader may here see at least one common wartime view of Stalin from the English/American side. Trotsky receives credit for his character and Stalin for his victories. Based mostly on secondary sources plus one interview.

A17. **Lyons, Eugene.** *Stalin, Czar of All the Russias.* Philadelphia: J. B. Lippincott, 1940, 292 p.

Eugene Lyons, an American journalist, spent six years in Russia and met and interviewed Stalin before writing this biography. Stalin is portrayed as amoral, and the book's overall tone is anti-Stalin. Emphasis is placed on changes in Russia since 1927. The work is built in part on Boris Souvarine's earlier book, *Stalin, A Critical Study of Bolshevism* [item A22]. This biography is of primary interest for its contemporary view of Stalin.

A18. **Marx-Engels-Lenin Institute.** *Joseph Stalin: A Short Biography.* Moscow: Foreign Languages Publishing House, 1980, 206 p.

An official biography, primarily a work of "Stalin Cult" literature written to help perpetuate the myths, legends and exaggerations surrounding Stalin. First issued in the late 1930s, this work may have been written in part by Stalin, but at the least was certainly approved by the dictator before publication. The reader should take little at face value in this book. This translation is based on the second, revised and enlarged, Russian edition.

A19. **Molotov, Vyacheslav Mikhaylovich, et al.** *Stalin.* New York: Workers Library Publishers, 1940, 190 p.

Similar in style to Yaroslavsky's 1940 *Landmarks in the Life of Stalin* [item A25], this title presents a variety of slavishly fawning essays written on the occasion of the ruler's 60th birthday. A sampling of authors (and chapters): Voroshilov ("Stalin, Builder of the Red Army"), Kaganovich ("The Great Driver of the Locomotive of History"), Mikoyan ("Stalin—The Lenin of Our Day"), Khrushchev ("Stalin and the Great Commonwealth of Nations") Beria ("The Greatest Man of Our Day"), Poskrebyshev ("Teacher and Friend of Mankind"), and Dimitroff ("Stalin and the World Proletariat"). An excellent example of the personality-cult engine operating in high gear.

A20. **Murphy, John Thomas.** *Stalin, 1879-1944.* London: John Lane, The Bodley Head, 1945, 251 p., bibliography.

A fairly admiring biography that tends to skip over such events as the Great Purge. Murphy writes that Stalin built a powerful economic and social system in which all multinational states and citizens had attained classless freedom and equality. The author believed that Stalin had fulfilled some of Abraham Lincoln's hopes regarding government of, by, and for the people (p. 240). For Murphy, then, Stalin had not betrayed Marx and Lenin, but had pragmatically perfected them in one country. Some of the praise and positive evaluation here may be put down to the desire to maintain wartime allegiances, but much of the book still reads like propaganda from *within* the Kremlin.

A21.   **Owen, Frank.** *The Three Dictators: Mussolini, Stalin, Hitler.* London: George Allen & Unwin, 1941, 266 p.

The last revised edition of *The Three Dictators* appeared in 1941 prior to the German strike at Russia, and the author refers to all three of his subjects as "ruffians" (p. 7, rev. 2nd ed.). He contends, however, that the dictators are not the main cause of their countries' suffering but rather an effect of same. Stalin is portrayed as a shrewd and scheming functionary who patiently undermined his often better-known opponents. The Stalinist economy, however, is pictured as inefficient and ripe for challenge. Something of a popular history.

A22.   **Souvarine, Boris.** *Stalin: A Critical Survey of Bolshevism.* New York: Alliance Book/Longmans Green, 1939, 690 p.

This biography is one of the pioneering early studies of Stalin and the Soviet Communist Party, and is considered one of the best analyses of Stalin at that relatively early date. Souvarine disliked Stalin but wrote a fairly balanced biography, although he was criticized at the time for being too antagonistic. The interpretations of events reflect Souvarine's Marxist background, for he was one of the founders of the French Communist Party.

A. BIOGRAPHIES, MEMOIRS, AND RELATED WORKS

A23.   **Stalin, Joseph, et al.** *Stalin: A Self-Portrait.* New York: Farrar, Straus and Young, 1953, unpaged.

A collection of photographs of Stalin along with quotes from his speeches and other writings.

A24.   **Tutaev, David,** ed. *The Alliluyev Memoirs: Recollections of Svetlana Stalina's Maternal Aunt Anna Alliluyeva and Her Grandfather Sergii Alliluyev.* New York: G. P. Putnam's Sons, 1968, 222 p., bibliography.

Shortly after publication in Russia, these memoirs of Stalin's sister-in-law and father-in-law were censored because some of the recollections did not match the official portraits of the "Cult." The Alliluyev family knew Stalin from pre-revolutionary days and were in a position to provide background material about his life. Unfortunately, as the compiler explains in the introduction, Stalin was angered by the original memoirs and had them doctored. The surviving results are of limited value, although the compiler's introduction offers valuable information about the precensored materials.

A25.   **Yaroslavsky, Emelian,** ed. *Landmarks in the Life of Stalin.* London: Lawrence & Wishart Ltd., 1942, 191 p.

Closely based upon the 1940 Moscow original edition, this title presents a version of the dictator's life that may seem highly sanitized and brazenly idolatrous to all but the most ardent Stalinists. The subject of the book is joined with Marx, Engels, and Lenin as "one of the outstanding geniuses of the human race" (p. 6, 1940 ed.). Needless to say, Stalin receives early credit as a leading figure of communism. His known disagreements with Lenin are almost invisible here, and Trotsky is depicted in a less than flattering light. See also *Stalin*, by Molotov and others (A19) for a corresponding group hosanna and a veritable veneration of the leader's military, political, social, and other accomplishments. These titles are excellent examples of Stalinist Cult literature.

BIOGRAPHIES AND MEMOIRS (AFTER 1953)

A26. Adams, Arthur E. *Stalin and His Times.* Prospect Heights, IL: Waveland Press, 1986, 243 p., bibliography.

Adams covers the 1923-53 period and argues that the Soviet Union's bootstrap industrialization and its emergence as a world power hold promise for undeveloped countries. Stalin's administrative skills and organizing mania are seen as the chief causes of his success and whatever excesses occurred. The author does not deny the organization of terror, but holds that both Russia and world communism benefitted on the whole from the dictator's overall program. Closes with a ten-page bibliographic essay.

A27A. Allilueva [i.e., Alliluyeva], Svetlana. *Only One Year.* New York: Harper & Row, 1969, 444 p.

A27B. Allilueva, Svetlana. *Twenty Letters to a Friend.* New York: Harper & Row, 1967, 246 p.

These two volumes record the memoirs of Stalin's daughter by his second marriage. Although reviews of the book were mixed, these remembrances still offer limited though valuable anecdotal insights into Stalin's personal life, as well as candid comments on many of the major political personalities in his inner circle. In *Twenty Letters* Beria is portrayed as an evil advisor exercising great influence over Stalin. Svetlana Alliluyeva defected to the West, where these memoirs were written.

A28. Antonov-Ovseenko, Anton. *The Time of Stalin: Portrait of a Tyranny.* New York: Harper & Row, 1981, 374 p., bibliography.

A personal and bitter work of accusation from an author who spent most of the 1940s trapped in the Gulag after his father had suffered death in the 1938 purge. Some startling statistics—such as a total death count of 100 million—are taken from sources such as the Khrushchev report, and the book also utilizes many anonymous and/or unpublished reminiscences. The somewhat hazy documentation methods may reduce the value to some as they read about various horrors from the mid-1920s through 1953; however, the Stalinistic system itself rather discouraged careful citations by historians.

A29. **Bortoli, Georges.** *The Death of Stalin.* New York: Praeger Publishers, 1975, 214 p., bibliography.

Dismissed by a number of reviewers as a superficial effort, this title makes heavy use of written reports by Svetlana Stalin and Nikita Khrushchev, but without much evaluation of its own. Due to the extremely paranoid nature of much Stalinist-era writing, one can not always expect careful documentation; however, Bortoli here may have crossed even the far boundaries of likelihood.

A30. **Bullock, Alan.** *Hitler and Stalin: Parallel Lives.* New York: Alfred A. Knopf, 1992, 1081 p., bibliography.

The well-known historian here studies the lives of Hitler and Stalin chronologically through the mid-1930s in alternating chapters, and then topically after 1934. Bullock compares the character, personality, political methods, and goals of both dictators and finds them much alike. The author is especially strong in showing how Hitler and Stalin understood power and how it is acquired. An interesting and scholarly study. The author's earlier work, *Hitler: A Study in Tyranny,* is a standard biography.

A31. **Cameron, Kenneth Neill.** *Stalin: Man of Contradiction.* Rev. ed. Toronto: NC Press, 1989, 203 p., bibliography.

This is a generally well balanced biography with some emphasis on Stalin's accomplishments and less emphasis on some of his negative contributions. Stalin is seen as a practical revolutionary whose importance should not be underestimated. Cameron compares the importance of Stalin's work with that of Trotsky and Bukharin during the Revolution and through the 1920s and 1930s. *Stalin: Man of Contradiction* provides a good analysis of the dictator's thought and philosophy.

A32.   **Conquest, Robert.** *Stalin: Breaker of Nations.* New York: Viking, 1991, 346 p., bibliography.

Conquest's provides a general biographical study of Stalin and a reexamination of Stalin's life and career based on the latest information released under glasnost. Although there are no startling new revelations, the author updates much old information and corrects some old misinformation. A readable and highly recommended introductory study.

A33.   **De Jonge, Alex.** *Stalin and the Shaping of the Soviet Union.* New York: William Morrow & Co., 1986, 542 p., bibliography.

A well written biography of Stalin that keeps the reader's attention. De Jonge contends that Stalin and his methods made the Soviet Union a superpower. An excellent synthesis of material from official sources, literature, and *emigré* writings, De Jonge's book is one of the better biographies of Stalin for the general reader.

A34.   **Ebon, Martin.** *Svetlana: The Story of Stalin's Daughter.* New York: New American Library, 1967, 216 p.

A thin biography with less material on Svetlana's father than might be expected, and rather more on other Russian history than might be desired.

A. BIOGRAPHIES, MEMOIRS, AND RELATED WORKS

A35A. Ehrenburg, Il'ia. *Memoirs, 1921-1941.* Cleveland: World Publishing Co., 1964, 543 p.

A35B. Ehrenburg, Il'ia. *Post-War Years, 1945-1954.* Cleveland: World Publishing Co., 1967, 349 p.

A35C. Ehrenburg, Il'ia. *The War, 1941-1945.* Cleveland: World Publishing Co., 1964, 198 p.

These three volumes covering the Stalin era are part of the author's six-volume autobiography. Ehrenburg is not considered a great writer; however, he knew most of the important writers and artists in the Soviet Union, and his memoirs offer useful insights into the climate of the Stalin years. Ehrenburg met and corresponded with Stalin and assisted in carrying out Stalin's policies, although perhaps not always willingly. In spite of not offering a great deal of new information on Stalin, these memoirs are useful for providing a Soviet review of the era.

A36A. Ginzburg, Evgeniia Semenovna. *Journey Into the Whirlwind.* New York: Harcourt, Brace & World, 1967, 418 p.

A36B. Ginzburg, Evgeniia Semenovna. *Within the Whirlwind.* New York: Harcourt Brace Jovanovich, 1981, 423 p.

Journey Into the Whirlwind is considered one of the best memoirs of the Stalin years. The author, an enthusiastic party member, was arrested in 1937 during the Stalin-Yezov party purges and was imprisoned and later exiled. The descriptions of the terror and its effect on the individual are graphic and moving. The sequel, *Within the Whirlwind*, covers Ginzburg's years of exile and rehabilitation. The English edition of *Journey* is titled *Into the Whirlwind*.

A37. Gorbatov, Aleksandr. *Years Off My Life: The Memoirs of General of the Soviet Army A. V. Gorbatov.* New York: W. W. Norton, 1965, 222 p.

23

A perhaps typical account of a military purge victim of the 1930s, except that Stalin's government later erased all charges and brought Gorbatov back from a convict gold mine in order to defend his country against the Germans. Some critics thought the author avoided any meaningful explanations of the housecleanings or the rehabilitations, but such evasiveness might have seemed quite natural and self-protective to other lucky survivors.

A38. **Grey, Ian.** *Stalin: Man of History.* Garden City, NY: Doubleday & Co., 1979, 547 p., bibliography.

Portrays the subject with some admiration as the latest in a long line of nationalistic Russian strongmen in the habitual mold of Ivan the Terrible and other czars. Gray maintains that Stalin played a more important part in the Revolution than he is credited with by some. He defends the dictator as not being wholly responsible for the Great Purge and as a man whose leadership vastly emboldened his country. The book contains a great deal of political as well as biographical material. Reviewers had mixed reactions to this title, due to some concern that Grey did not seem more critical of Stalin's harsher domestic policies.

A39. **Gromyko, Andrei Andreevich.** *Memoirs.* New York: Doubleday, 1990, 414 p.

There is not much on Stalin in these accounts, although the book remains interesting primarily as an illustration of how a typical Soviet diplomat provides concrete examples of the narrow rigidity of foreign policy under Stalin. Gromyko was Ambassador to the United States starting in 1940, and continuing into the modern period.

A40. **Harriman, W. Averell,** and **Elie Abel.** *Special Envoy to Churchill and Stalin, 1941-1946.* New York: Random House, 1975, 595 p.

Harriman acted as the U.S. Ambassador to the Soviet Union from 1943-46 and had numerous encounters and dealings with Stalin. The dictator puzzled the envoy, who alternated between modest optimism and some pessimism in his hopes for ongoing entente with Russia. Harriman did not really decide on Stalin's personality, but did believe that deep-seated suspicion of the West played a big part in Stalin's actions and policies. Critics generally welcomed this memoir; however, a similar effort by George F. Kennan, Harriman's assistant for a time, received higher accolades as a more thoughtful work.

A41. **Hingley, Ronald.** *Joseph Stalin: Man and Legend.* New York: McGraw-Hill Book Co., 1974, 482 p., bibliography.

Tries to separate the man from the myth, although some reviewers felt that Hingley perpetrates certain fables and ignores important facts. The author contends that Stalin's Marxist biographers have discounted or dismissed his real accomplishments—such as the construction of a great Soviet state from its unstable Leninist beginnings—due to his alleged betrayal of pure communism.

A42. **Hoxha, Enver.** *With Stalin: Memoirs.* 2nd. ed. Tirana, Albania: "8 Nentori" Publishing House, 1981, 223 p.

Details the Albanian dictator's Moscow visits with Stalin between 1947 and 1951. Hoxha denounced the crimes of Stalin at a 1956 Albanian party congress, but the present volume idealizes the Soviet leader and actually places guilt for purge excesses on subordinates such as Khrushchev. The author admits with pride that he and Stalin did kill some traitors. Hoxha portrays his Georgian hero as a principled man, a rare and true communist, and one too compassionate to be a tyrant. Hoxha was himself discredited after the fall of the Communist regime in Albania in the early 1990s.

A43. **Hutton, Joseph Bernard.** *Stalin, The Miraculous Georgian.* London: Neville Spearman, 1961, 375 p., bibliography.

Portrays Stalin as something of a god to his people, but also as a man who poisoned both Lenin and his own wife and was perhaps perfectly ruthless. Hutton alleges from accounts by Beria and Ehrenburg that Molotov actually gave his boss a glass of poisoned brandy after an accident on 1 March 1953, and that this led to the dictator's passing on 5 March. The writer spent 1934-38 in Moscow as a Czech-born editor of a Russian newspaper. He claims to have travelled extensively throughout the Soviet Union at the time and to have uncovered misplaced or officially "undiscovered" copies of books by Lenin and others that have since been suppressed.

A44. **Hyde, H. Montgomery.** *Stalin: The History of a Dictator.* New York: Da Capo Press, 1982, 679 p., bibliography.

A readable effort that tries to reconcile two different pictures of Stalin...one the Allied "comrade" of the early 1940s with some warmth, and the other a cold sadist of a man who brazenly undercut the communist revolution and slaughtered millions of his own people. Hyde is not alone in failing to completely bridge the gap. Some reviewers went further, however, and accused the author of a sloppy and inconsistent use of sources. Originally published in 1971.

A45. **Kahan, Stuart.** *The Wolf of the Kremlin.* New York: William Morrow & Co., 1987, 331 p., bibliography.

This title is based centrally on an alleged 1981 conversation in Moscow with Lazar Kaganovich, the author's uncle and a leading commissar of industry. Kahan claims that Kaganovich earned the "Wolf" nickname as Stalin's behind-the-scenes coordinator of all terror, that he often showed no mercy for fellow Jews, that he was a close confidant of the ruler, and that his rise to Politburo Chair made him second in power for a time. Kaganovich is described as one of a shadow cabinet who planned the poisoning of their leader. Stalin is shown as highly suspicious, sometimes unstable, and instinctively cunning. This book has a brief bibliography but no footnotes. Critics greeted the publication with some doubts as to its complete veracity.

A46A. **Khrushchev, Nikita Sergeevich.** *Khrushchev Remembers.* Boston: Little, Brown & Co., 1970, 639 p.
A46B. **Khrushchev, Nikita Sergeevich.** *Khrushchev Remembers: The Last Testament.* Boston: Little, Brown & Co., 1974, 602 p.
A46C. **Khrushchev, Nikita Sergeevich.** *Khrushchev Remembers: The Glasnost Tapes.* Boston: Little, Brown & Co., 1990, 219 p.

This trilogy comprises the memoirs of Nikita Khrushchev, who succeeded to head the Soviet state soon after Stalin's death. When these memoirs were first published in the West, doubt arose as to their authenticity. Today those doubts have been eased, and the memoirs have been accepted as authentic. The first volume includes most of the material on Stalin and on the rise of Beria's influence on Stalin. The second volume is concerned primarily with the post-war years. The final volume has some new materials on Stalin's charisma and his hold over Soviet leaders. Reflecting on Khruschev's life through these volumes may also illustrate something important about Stalin, since it was the latter who undoubtedly allowed the former to survive and prosper. Includes a copy of Khrushchev's closed speech of 1956 that denounced his former patron.

A47. **Laqueur, Walter.** *Stalin: The Glasnost Revelations.* New York: Charles Scribner's Sons, 1990, 382 p., bibliography.

Laqueur's study is a reevaluation of Stalin's political career and the development of Stalinism based on documents and information made available under Gorbachev's glasnost policy. The work is especially valuable for its reexamination of Soviet historiography and Soviet opinion of Stalin. The new information corrects a number of errors; however, no major revelations came to light.

A48. **Levine, Isaac Don.** *Stalin's Great Secret.* New York: Coward-McCann, 1956, 126 p.

This book was also appeared as *Stalin Was a Tsarist Agent,* a title which better summarizes Levine's somewhat controversial thesis. To some observers, czarist connections even for pragmatic purposes of survival would seem unlikely for one of the Soviet founders. On the other hand, Stalin's propensity for incredible double-dealing within the party might support the idea that he could at least have betrayed a few early comrades to the Okhrana for monetary and/or self-survival reasons. Perhaps Levine's somewhat questionable documentary evidence will find better substantiation or convincing renunciation from the opening of certain KGB files in 1992 or later.

A49. **Lewin, Moshe.** *Lenin's Last Struggle.* New York: Monthly Review Press, 1978, 193 p., bibliography.

A noted scholar of Soviet history has written this specialized study about Lenin's concerns and thoughts on leadership of the Communist Party after his death. Lewin emphasizes Lenin's consideration of Stalin and Trotsky as his successors. Chapter 6, "Lenin's Testament," is of special interest because of materials on Lenin's concern about Stalin's personality and the Stalin-Trotsky split. The book also contains an analysis of Lenin's thoughts on other important contemporary Soviet leaders—Zinoviev, Kamenev, Bukharin, and Pyatakov.

A50. **Lewis, Jonathan, and Phillip Whitehead.** *Stalin: A Time for Judgment.* New York: Pantheon Books, 1990, 254 p., bibliography.

This well written, fast paced biography is an excellent introduction for the general reader. The authors present a balanced study based on written sources, numerous personal interviews, and extensive travels in the Soviet Union. Over 100 illustrations, many published for the first time, enhance the text. The book is a companion to the PBS television series on Stalin.

A51. **Litvinov, Maxim.** *Notes for a Journal.* London: André Deutsch, 1955, 303 p.

This alleged journal records the memories of a man involved intermittently with Soviet foreign policy and with Stalin's inner court from 1926 to 1950. Litvinov demonstrates some loyalty to his master and suggests that Stalin began secret dealings with Germany around two years prior to the 1939 non-aggression pact. Reviewers found *Notes* quite readable, but some doubted its complete authenticity.

A52. **Maisky, Ivan.** *Memoirs of a Soviet Ambassador: The War, 1939-43.* New York: Charles Scribner's Sons, 1968, 408 p.

The author served as the Ambassador to Great Britain from 1932-1943 and made widespread contacts there in spite of his own devotion to communism. Maisky's diplomacy aided the U.S.S.R. during 1940 when he first tried to warn Stalin of Hitler's impending threat, and later, after the German attack, when he lobbied the British for monetary and military support. Stalin is criticized for his treaty with Hitler and for his peremptory treatment of envoys. Maisky should also have suspected his leader's distrust of Soviet Jews working abroad, and the author fit the category. He may well have thought that Stalin had swayed too far from doctrinal purity toward personal power.

A53. **McCauley, Martin.** *Stalin and Stalinism.* Harlow, England: Longman, 1983, 128 p., bibliography.

McCauley summarizes the life of Stalin and his use of government, and also provides extracts of documents by Stalin and others along with a glossary. The author maintains that the dictator kept control by watching and manipulating the party, the government, and the secret police. He recognizes Stalinism's systematic use of terror, but asserts that the mass industrialization of the 1930s allowed the Soviet Union to withstand the German attack in World War II. Other writers may believe that the sheer magnitude of Soviet resources, in company perhaps with some outside help, eventually brought Soviet survival and victory *in spite of* Stalinist inefficiencies.

A54. **McNeal, Robert Hatch.** *Stalin: Man and Ruler.* New York: New York University Press, 1988, 389 p., bibliography.

Penned by an historian who has written several monographs and articles on Stalin and has edited certain volumes of the dictator's works, this title attempts partially to demythologize and humanize its subject. McNeal uses some material perhaps unavailable to earlier biographers in covering the main events and in discussing such traits as Stalin's sense of humor and his supposed religious beliefs in the early years. One of his larger claims has Stalin playing a palliative role in the collectivization drive of the late 1920s.

A55. **Medvedev, Roy Aleksandrovich.** *All Stalin's Men.* New York: Anchor Press/Doubleday, 1984, 184 p., bibliography.

A reflection of Stalin's suspicious and yet maladroit mind through the careers of six of his most influential and yet

unremarkable assistants: Kaganovich, Malenkov, Mikoyan, Molotov, Suslov, and Voroshilov. None of the six
were liquidated, and all but Suslov—a leading communist
ideologue—survived Stalin. Medvedev described this
group as "grey figures" who set aside morals, family, and
friends for power.

A56. **Nicolaevsky, Boris I.** *Power and the Soviet Elite: "The
Letter of an Old Bolshevik," and Other Essays.* New
York: Praeger Publishers, 1965, 275 p.

The primary interest in this volume is the essay, "The
Letter of an Old Bolshevik," and the related materials on
the plan to replace Stalin in 1936. Stalin was to be given
a title but was to retain no real power. The plan, of
course, failed.

A57. **Payne, Robert.** *The Rise and Fall of Stalin.* New York:
Simon & Schuster, 1965, 864 p., bibliography.

Payne's long biography builds extensively on materials
released by Khrushchev in and after his 1956 "secret
speech." This reliance may weaken the book's credibility
to the extent that Khrushchev's own propaganda deviated
from the actual historical events. Payne moderately asserts that Stalin poisoned Lenin, and was in turn murdered some thirty years later by disaffected Politburo
members. Some critics have called the premise of this
book weak, because its conclusions rest on supposedly
doubtful or unproved details, while other reviewers think
that Payne has risen above certain specific shortcomings
to faithfully portray the overall essence of Stalin.

A58. **Pomper, Philip.** *Lenin, Trotsky, and Stalin: The Intelligentsia and Power.* New York: Columbia University
Press, 1990, 446 p., bibliography.

A psychobiographical account that first investigates the
early lives of the subjects and then devotes some thirty
pages of concentrated material to Stalin. Pomper uses the

personality models developed in order to explain subsequent political events through Lenin's death in 1924 and the start of Trotsky's demise. He portrays a Stalin who is anti-semitic and brutally expedient, a man with an abiding conviction in the proletariat cause and a deep belief in himself. The author also posits the idea that some of the horrors of 1929-53 trace back to jealousy of and insecurity about the greater parts played by Lenin, Trotsky, and others in 1917.

A59. Rancour-Laferrière, Daniel. *The Mind of Stalin: A Psychoanalytic Study.* Ann Arbor, MI: Ardis, 1988, 161 p., bibliography.

This book is "a psychoanalytic investigation of selected, arrested behaviors in Stalin, from childhood to old age"—Preface. The author's central theme shows how Stalin's psychological development and his psychological state affected his public role and political decisions. The study focuses secondarily on Stalin's sadism and vindictiveness. The author sees Stalin's paranoia and feelings of inferiority as the cause of the terror of the 1930s and later. The topics covered include: "The Surface Structure of the Dictator's Psyche," "Beating the Children of Russia," and "The Homosexual Element." Rancour-Laferrière is a professor of Russian at the University of California, Davis.

A60. Rigby, Thomas Henry, ed. *Stalin.* Englewood Cliffs, NJ: Prentice-Hall, 1966, 182 p., bibliography.

A book of excerpts and short pieces from Stalin himself as well as those who interacted with him. The selections aim to outline both personality and accomplishments, with the editor adding a bit of interpretation. Presents a wide panorama of samples, although the items may not individually represent much that is new or collectively represent any new appraisals of the dictator.

A. Biographies, Memoirs, and Related Works

A61. **Romano-Petrova, N.** *Stalin's Doctor, Stalin's Nurse: A Memoir.* Princeton, NJ: Kingston Press, 1984.

Based on an alleged diary kept by Dr. Pletnev, a heart specialist supposedly serving—until his arrest in 1938—as one of Stalin's most trusted physicians, *Stalin's Doctor* includes stories that Stalin personally murdered his second wife and caused Maxim Gorky's death. These unsubstantiated tales generally demonstrate the ruler's reported anti-semitism and crude behavior. The twenty-five-page introduction provides background information as well as speculation on the main section's verisimilitude. No sources are really documented, which makes this yet another source of Stalinistic rumor—true or false or mixed.

A62. **Shostakovich, Dmitrii Dmitrievich.** *Testimony: The Memoirs of Dmitri Shostakovich.* New York: Harper & Row, 1979, 289 p.

A wandering reminiscence describing the paranoid life of this Soviet musician, who felt that he only just managed to avoid the same Stalinistic scythe that cut down so many other artists. Shostakovich writes of his dealings with the superstitious dictator and of how certain people became toadies, while others adopted an ironic and dangerous working style. The author gained fame as a musical genius, but finally lost his assurance in Soviet society.

A63. **Slusser, Robert M.** *Stalin in October: The Man Who Missed the Revolution.* Baltimore: Johns Hopkins University Press, 1987, 281 p., bibliography.

The focus of this study is Stalin's part in leading the 1917 revolution between March and October of that year. Slusser accounts in detail for Stalin's activities and relationships with Lenin, Trotsky, and other leaders during this critical period. The conclusion is that Stalin played only a minor role in the revolution. Later this was to play a part in the purges, when contemporary witnesses were killed as the Stalin Cult developed and history was rewritten.

A64. **Smith, Edward Ellis.** *The Young Stalin: The Early Years of an Elusive Revolutionary.* New York: Farrar, Straus and Giroux, 1968, 470 p., bibliography.

Smith argues that Stalin's many close escapes from and his possibly benign treatment from the Czarist police point inevitably to some hidden cooperation between the two. The book makes use of certain Okhrana files taken eventually to the Hoover Institution. Although the materials cited may not always provide clear and incontrovertible evidence, the author does make a strong and logical thesis based upon repeated coincidences and similar evidence.

A65. **Tremain, Rose.** *Stalin.* New York: Ballantine Books, 1975, 159 p., bibliography.

A brief, popular history filled with many black-and-white photographs, *Stalin* views the dictator's paranoid and heartless adult behavior and some of his revolutionary impulse as reactions to the cruelty of his father and the general poverty of his childhood. The author recognizes the leader's responsibility for certain harsh and inhumane policies, but also emphasizes the argument that forced modernization appeared truly necessary to Stalin. He needed to build up the U.S.S.R., in other words, so that it could survive such threats as the spread of Nazi Germany. Tremain acknowledges that political tyranny rather than ideological conviction served as a prime motive for Stalin; but she also maintains that he was, by and large, loved by the Soviet people in spite of their widespread suffering under his government. ·

A66. **Tucker, Robert C.** *Stalin As Revolutionary, 1879-1929: A Study in History and Personality.* New York: W. W. Norton & Co., 1973, 519 p., bibliography.

The focus of this biography is to show the "rendezvous of a personality with the public political world," and how that life was interwoven with the history of an era."—Preface. In many interpretations of Stalin's actions, Tucker uses psychohistorical techniques to good effect. An excellent introductory work, *Stalin as Revolutionary* was the first part of a projected three-volume biography of Stalin. The second volume, *Stalin in Power: The Revolution From Above, 1928-1941* [item A67], was published in 1991.

A67. **Tucker, Robert C.** *Stalin in Power: The Revolution from Above, 1928-1941.* New York: W. W. Norton & Co., 1991, 707 p., bibliography.

The central theme of this biography is Stalin's revolution from above, the so-called second revolution, in which the state carried out such radical reforms as collectivization. Tucker's book shows "how and why this second revolution took place, how it developed in stages, and with what consequences, and what parts Stalin and others played in it and why."—Preface. This is the second part of a projected three-volume biography, the first being *Stalin as Revolutionary* [item A66], with the third yet to appear. The set received generally excellent reviews, and is one of the best comprehensive biographies of Stalin currently available.

A68. **Tuominen, Arvo.** *The Bells of the Kremlin: An Experience in Communism.* Hanover, CT: University Press of New England, 1983, 333 p.

Tuominen's autobiographical work provides many new insights into Stalin and the other Soviet leaders. The author, a former General Secretary of the Finnish Communist Party, observed Stalin personally, and writes from this direct experience. The material on the terror and purges of the 1930s is noteworthy. Tuominen broke with the party in 1935. Based on personal interviews and parts of his other writings.

A69. **Ulam, Adam B.** *Stalin: The Man and His Era.* Boston: Beacon Press, 1989, 760 p.

This long book explores the history of the Bolshevik party, the Russian Revolution, and Soviet government in relation to its chief leader from 1924-53. *Stalin* portrays the Georgian as something of an original tool of Lenin's and as one who eventually far surpassed his sponsor's scope of power. Ulam does not absolve Stalin of all blame for the terror of his reign, but apportions some responsibility to the others around him. He also argues that the dictator operated with precise, complex political moves that belie any picture of him as a boorish, psychopathic hack, and contends that Western diplomats during World War II were generally hoodwinked by the Russian leader and that Stalinism had not really died out even twenty years after its founder's demise. The lack of a bibliography may be a small demerit here, although footnotes do appear. This edition has a second introduction but otherwise reprints the 1973 Viking original.

A70. **Volkogonov, Dmitrii Antonovich.** *Stalin: Triumph and Tragedy.* New York: Grove Weidenfeld, 1991, 642 p., bibliography.

The author, head of the Institute of Military History, has written a balanced biography of Stalin that is especially important because it is an attempt by a Soviet historian to come to terms with Stalin. The overall assessment of Stalin is negative, but he is credited for industrializing the Soviet Union and making it a military power. Volkogonov believes Stalin rejected socialism and was against freedom for the masses. The work is an important advance in Soviet historiography of the period.

A71. **Warth, Robert D.** *Joseph Stalin.* New York: Twayne Publishers, 1969, 176 p., bibliography.

A good summary work without any unusual conclusions, *Joseph Stalin* features a helpful bibliographical essay for further research. Warth is a reputable scholar in the field of Russian studies.

A72. **Wolfe, Bertram D.** *Three Who Made a Revolution: A Biographical History.* 4th rev. ed. New York: Stein and Day, 1984, 659 p.

Well-known writer Wolfe describes the early years of Lenin, Trotsky, and Stalin prior to the 1917 revolution, portraying the young Dzhugashvili as more of a local/provincial figure in Russian Bolshevism until 1907, whereas the offical histories published in Russia tend to award him national or even international status at a much earlier date. Wolfe was an acquaintance of both Stalin and Trotsky who later worked as an analyst for the U.S. State Department. This standard text was first published in 1948, being quite well received by the critics, and has been reprinted here from the fourth revised edition of 1964.

A73. **Wolman, Benjamin B., ed.** *The Psychoanalytic Interpretation of History.* New York: Basic Books, 1971, 240 p., bibliography.

This volume is one of the seminal studies using psychoanalysis to analyze and interpret the actions of individuals as well as to explain certain aspects of art and literature. There are several essays explaining the "psychohistorical approach" as well as essays on Hitler and Stalin. Gustav Bychowski, a professor of psychiatry, wrote the section on Stalin, "Joseph V. Stalin: Paranoia and the Dictatorship of the Proletariat." The psychohistorical method is interesting, but it has been subjected to criticism and must be approached cautiously.

A74. **Zhukov, Georgi K.** *The Memoirs of Marshal Zhukov.* New York: Delacorte Press, 1971, 703 p.

The reminiscenses of one of the Soviet Union's top generals during the Great Patriotic War of 1941-45 attempt to reglorify Stalin following the anti-Stalinist Khrushchev years. Some critics felt that this volume represented Zhukov's party-line effort to regain a spot on the Politburo, and that its author had displayed little martial creativity and even less human warmth. Readers may or may not agree with these criticisms, but will still find noteworthy material in Zhukov's military, political, and personal closeups of Stalin.

TROTSKY'S WRITINGS ABOUT STALIN

A75. **Trotsky, Leon.** *On the Suppressed Testament of Lenin.* 3rd ed. New York: Pathfinder Press, 1970, 47 p.

A biased but carefully crafted review of the philosophical and administrative disagreements between Lenin and Stalin. This rift led to Lenin's purported, final written recommendation that the Party must remove Stalin from his General Secretary position. Trotsky claims that Lenin thought Stalin was a "revolutionist" with martial tenacity but was not enough of a "statesman" (p. 20). Furthermore, it is alleged that Lenin lost moral faith in the Georgian protégé who had schemed his way past the role of a mere bureaucratic organizer. Trotsky also takes a vicious swipe at the Stalinist biographer, Emil Ludwig.

A76. **Trotsky, Leon.** *The Real Situation in Russia.* New York: Harcourt, Brace & Co., 1928, 364 p.

This early, searing indictment of Stalin and his methods was penned by the talented polemicist and possibly inept politician who would—according to many reports—eventually die at his enemy's directive. Some reviewers at the time wondered whether this book really described the true status quo; and, given the surreal appearance of communist history to certain non-believers, who can honestly say even today? In any case, Trotsky writes with great force and conviction.

A77. Trotsky, Leon. *The Revolution Betrayed: What Is the Soviet Union and Where Is It Going?* Garden City, NY: Doubleday, Doran & Co., 1937, 308 p.

Another in the author's contemporaneous series of vitriolic denunciations of Stalin. Trotsky argues that the Soviet leader abandoned the true political and economic gospel of Lenin and Marx.

A78. Trotsky, Leon. *Stalin: An Appraisal of the Man and His Influence.* New York: Stein & Day, 1970, 516 p.

Originally published 1941, this book was never completely finished by the author—due to his assassination in 1940, supposedly on Stalin's orders. Several editions appeared from 1946 through the 1960s. About half the work comes from unfinished notes and fragments. Trotsky paints his subject and great antagonist as a dishonest schemer, and provides first-hand views from before and after the Revolution. The writing style and value drew widely variant comments from the critics. Despite or perhaps because of the author's personal involvement and emotional venom, this title should always have an important place among primary Stalinist sources.

A79. Trotsky, Leon. *The Stalin School of Falsification.* 3rd ed. New York: Pathfinder Press, 1972, 338 p.

At the time this work first appeared in 1937, the writer had been largely expunged in all but the physical sense from the Russian political scene. Trotsky accuses Stalin of grossly altering source documents for personal benefit and to bring scorn upon the true Marxist disciples. Penned with typical Trotsky power and bile, *The Stalin School* speaks out loudly about the excesses of the Russian dictator, although some contemporaneous critics may have underrated its value until its author's untimely demise just a few years later. Many historians believe that Stalin personally ordered Trotsky's assassination; if so, the present volume could well have represented another nail driven by the author into his own coffin.

A80. **Matlock, Jack F.** *An Index to the Collected Works of J. V. Stalin.* New York: Johnson Reprint Corporation, 1971, 192 p.

This index to the Russian edition of Stalin's collected works can also be used with the English translation because the paging corresponds closely. Originally published in 1955 as *External Research Paper, no. 118* by the Office of Intelligence Research, Department of State.

A81. **McNeal, Robert Hatch.** *Stalin's Works: An Annotated Bibliography.* Stanford, CA: Hoover Institution on War, Revolution and Peace, 1967, 197 p.

This is the standard bibliography on Stalin's writings. Over 895 items are cited, including early poems and later writings through 1952. An introductory section explains what is included and the difficulties involved in determining authentic materials. This work compliments Matlock's *Index to the Collected Works of J. V. Stalin* [item A80].

A82. **Stalin, Joseph.** *The Essential Stalin: Major Theoretical Writings, 1905-1952.* Garden City, NY: Anchor Books, Doubleday & Co., 1972, 511 p.

A good collection of Stalin's written work covering his active years as a revolutionary and later as dictator. The introduction is controversial and has been criticized by reviews because the editor presents a strong pro-Stalin view.

A83. **Stalin, Joseph.** *Marxism and Linguistics.* New York: International Publishers, 1951, 63 p.

25

This slim volume is Stalin's sole foray into linguistics, now of interest only as a curiosity. The book proves only that dictators should stay away from scholarly fields outside their areas of expertise.

A84. **Stalin, Joseph.** *Problems of Leninism.* Moscow: Foreign Languages Publishing House, 1953, 803 p.

First published in 1926, this volume has probably had more impact than any of Stalin's other writings. The book has been called "the standard anthology of Stalinism," and helped to establish Stalin's role as an interpreter of communist ideology. *Problems of Leninism* was used to enhance Stalin's reputation as a critical thinker. This book is a collection of materials and not a single work. The first edition numbered under 100 pages, compared to over 800 pages in this version, which is based on the 11th edition also published in Moscow.

A85. **Stalin, Joseph.** *Selected Works.* Davis, CA: Cardinal Publishers, 1971, 393 p., bibliography.

A selection of Stalin's more important works. The materials are presented in four sections: "Basic Principles of Marxism-Leninism," "The National Question," "Socialist Revolution and Social Construction," and "Other Topics."

A86. **Stalin, Joseph.** *Stalin's Kampf: Joseph Stalin's Credo Written by Himself.* New York: Howell, Soskin, 1940, 358 p., bibliography.

This collection of speeches and excerpts from Stalin's writings includes a good introduction, with sources given for each item.

A87. **Stalin, Joseph.** *Works.* Moscow: Foreign Languages Publishing House, 1952-55, 13 vols.

This is the official English-language edition of Stalin's writings prepared by the Marx-Engels-Lenin Institute of the Central Committee. Works written between 1901 and January 1934 are included. When Stalin died in 1953, work on the set was stopped and has not been restarted. The set is not complete even for 1901-1934, since some materials were excluded for political reasons and other works included were altered in some cases to fit current political circumstances or to rewrite history. Robert H. McNeal did complete the work by editing volumes 14-17 (*Sochineniia*. Stanford: Hoover Institution, 1967), but did not translate the materials into English.

For more information about the *Works* see Robert H. McNeal, *Stalin's Works: An Annotated Bibliography* [item A81] and Jack Matlock, *An Index to the Collected Works of J. V. Stalin* [item A80].

B.

STALINISM

GENERAL WORKS

B1. **Ali, Tariq**, ed. *The Stalinist Legacy: Its Impact on Twentieth Century World Politics.* New York: Penguin Books, 1984, 551 p., bibliography.

This anthology of essays on Stalinism from the Marxist/socialist point of view includes contributions by Trotsky, Deutscher, Tito, and others who do not share the philosophies on totalitarianism found among many Western writers. Also reprinted is Khrushchev's 1956 report to the 20th congress of the C.P.S.U. Topics covered include: U.S.S.R. social relations; Trotsky on Stalinism; Lenin's connection; the positions of literature and science; Stalin and World War II; and communism in Vietnam, India, China, and Albania. This book concentrates on politics more than economics or pure philosophy. Stalinism generally emerges here as a conservative force blocking the development of true socialist democracy.

B2. **Avtorkhanov, Abdurakhman.** *The Reign of Stalin.* Westport, CT: Hyperion Press, 1975, 256 p.

A history professor and party propagandist with Bukharinist leanings, Avtorkhanov writes with the perspective of one who watched his Chechen ethnic roots destroyed by the U.S.S.R., and who was arrested both by the N.K.V.D. and the Gestapo. This work concentrates on the purges, the kolkhoz program, the structuring of poverty, and the hypermanagement of news. A dialectic work perhaps more than a descriptive book, *The Reign of Stalin* fails to cite the origins of most of its information. The author used the name Alexander Uralov for the 1953 first edition. Translated from the French.

B3.   Boffa, Giuseppe. *The Stalin Phenomenon.* Ithaca, NY: Cornell University Press, 1992, 205 p., bibliography.

Boffa reviews a variety of historical and political inter-pretations of Stalinism: as a continuation of Marxism-Leninism, as a form of Russian reprisal, as a totalitarian system opposed to freedom and similar in ways to fas-cism, as an amplified version of statism, etc. The author also presents his own description of each system or phe-nomenon. He sees Stalinism as springing from Marxism-Leninism, divorcing its idealizations, but continuing to use its tenets as an ideological heart. Boffa notes that the extreme centralization of all economic and political life that characterized Stalinism also encompassed a reaction to capitalism, a desire for some radical new means of production and distribution, and at the same time some-thing of a return to rationalism. The author almost par-allels Stalinism with communism, but does not really equate the two. Translated and revised from the 1982 Italian original.

B4.   Butenko, Anatolii Pavlovich. *The Stalin Phenomenon: Soviet Scholars on the Sources of the Deviations from Socialism, the Causes of the Deformation in the Mecha-nism of Power Linked with the Personality Cult.* Moscow: Novosti Press Agency Publishing House, 1988, 63 p.

An analysis of the Stalin personality cult by contemporary Soviet scholars, *The Stalin Phenomenon* is an early revi-sionist work made possible under Gorbachev's glasnost policies. The selections in this collection represent an attempt by Soviet academics at an honest reinterpretation of the Stalin era.

B5. **Campeanu, Pavel.** *The Genesis of the Stalinist Social Order.* Armonk, NY: M. E. Sharpe, 1988, 165 p.

This scholarly work is a sociological analysis of the origins of Stalinism from a socialist perspective. The author identifies the state's ownership of property as central to Stalinism—Stalin expropriated property and upset the social and economic system. The Stalinist social order is seen as a failure held together by terror. The work is primarily for the advanced student.

B6. **Campeanu, Pavel.** *The Origins of Stalinism: From Leninist Revolution to Stalinist Society.* Armonk, NY: M. E. Sharpe, 1986, 187 p.

Compeanu's scholarly treatise is concerned primarily with the question of whether or not Stalinism was a logical and natural outcome of the 1917 revolution and Lenin's policies. The author argues that theoretical—not practical—economics combined with a stagnant bureaucracy led to Stalinism. Campeanu also wrote an earlier and more general study, *The Syncretic Society* (1980).

B7. **Carr, Edward Hallett.** *A History of Soviet Russia.* New York: Macmillan, 1950-78, 14 vols., bibliography.

This standard comprehensive history of Soviet Russia includes some material on Stalin, but the work is cited here primarily for its comprehensiveness. The volumes on "Socialism in One Country" and "Foundations of a Planned Economy" cover in part the years of Stalin's rise to power. A one-volume abridged edition, *The Russian Revolution from Lenin to Stalin* (New York: Free Press, 1979), is also useful.

B8. **Cassinelli, C. W.** *Total Revolution: A Comparative Study of Germany Under Hitler, the Soviet Union Under Stalin, and China Under Mao.* Santa Barbara, CA: Clio Books, 1976, 252 p.

Cassinelli contends that all three leaders utilized ideology to support efforts to completely rebuild their country's political, economic, and social systems. He also compares the reluctance of both Lenin and Stalin to delegate any power. Some critics felt that Cassinelli overplays philosophy and underplays practicalities, and that he allows his anti-communist bias to undermine the rationality of his thesis. Further comparison between Hitler and Stalin can be found in the works of Brzezinski.

B9. **Cohen, Stephen F.** *Rethinking the Soviet Experience: Politics and History Since 1917.* Oxford: Oxford University Press, 1985, 222 p., bibliography.

Cohen, a noted scholar of Soviet history, has written an excellent overview of recent Soviet history with an emphasis on Stalin and his policies. Representative sections of the book include: "Bolshevism and Stalinism," "Bukharin, NEP, and the Idea of an Alternative to Stalin," and "The Stalin Question Since Stalin."

B10. **Dallin, Alexander, and Bertrand M. Patenaude, eds.** *Stalin and Stalinism.* New York: Garland Publishing Co., 1992, 393 p.

This collection of important scholarly articles "...offers a survey of Western and Soviet interpretations of the Stalin era, presenting conflicting scholarly views on Stalin's rise to power and his turbulent rule—notably the revolution from above in 1929, and the great terror of the 1930s."—Publisher's note. Materials are organized and presented in six sections: "The State of the Field," "Bolshevism, Leninism, Stalinism," "Stalin's Career," "Reconsiderations and Revisions," "Stalinism: Western Perspective," and "Stalinism: Soviet Perspectives." A useful collection of materials which would be difficult to locate in their original sources.

B11. Dallin, David J. *From Purge to Coexistence: Essays on Stalin's and Khruschev's Russia.* Chicago: Henry Regnery Co., 1964, 289 p., bibliography.

A collection of essays by a Menshevik expatriate, *From Purge to Coexistence* ranges from the Great Purge to the failure in Austria to predictions of Chinese supremacy. A number of the pieces were written well before the book's 1964 publication date. The author likens Stalin to an unlettered Mongol imbued with technology (p. 173) who marched backwards from true Marxism for thirty years.

B12. Daniels, Robert Vincent, ed. *The Stalin Revolution: Foundations of the Totalitarian Era.* 3rd ed. Lexington, MA: D. C. Heath, 1990, 269 p., bibliography.

Daniels's anthology of essays by prominent scholars gives an overview of Stalin's policies and the events leading to the establishment of his dictatorship. The editor's introduction provides a unifying theme for the selections, and defines the historiographical problems involved in writing objectively about Stalin. The materials are presented in four sections: "The Setting," "The Revolution from Above," "The Counterrevolution from Above," and "Interpretations."

B13. Daniels, Robert Vincent. *Trotsky, Stalin, and Socialism.* Boulder, CO: Westview Press, 1991, 208 p., bibliography.

Trotsky, Stalin, and Socialism uses a number of footnoted essays by Daniels (a Slavic Studies professor who spent over thirty years at the University of Vermont) to trace the early course of communism and two of its bitterly differing protagonists. The author argues that Stalinism grew into cultural counterrevolution and represented a "contradiction of theory and practice" (p. ix). Stalin is portrayed as one concerned heavily with the vision of "his own personal glory" (p. 125), a man who legalized his dictatorship with the raiments of Marxism-Leninism.

B14. **Deutscher, Isaac.** *Russia After Stalin.* London: Jonathan Cape, 1969, 174 p.

First published in 1953 (and also in the United States as *Russia, What Next?*), this reprint includes a new introduction attached to the same original text. Deutscher argues that Malenkov inherited a self-destructive system upon Stalin's death and that democratic socialism would inevitably evolve. He also asserts that the Soviet Union's semi-colonial expansion after 1945 occurred against Stalin's wishes. The exploration of the despot's Georgian background and how those cultural experiences shaped him offer a good analysis of Stalin's roots and goals.

B15. **Elleinstein, Jean.** *The Stalin Phenomenon.* London: Lawrence and Wishart, 1976, 221 p., bibliography.

The author acts as apologist for purist Marxism by arguing that Stalinism represented a terrible exception to—and not the natural result of—socialist evolution. Stalin is therefore seen as an abnormality rather than a norm for models of communist leadership. Elleinstein believed that Stalinism was fading and that democracy could work as part of true communism.

B16. **Fainsod, Merle.** *How Russia Is Ruled.* Rev. ed. Cambridge, MA: Harvard University Press, 1963, 684 p., bibliography.

Fainsod's book attempts "...to analyse the physiology, as well as the anatomy, of Soviet totalitarianism and to communicate a sense of the living political processes in which Soviet rulers and subjects are enmeshed"—Preface. Of course, much responsibility for the construction and character of this system may be attributed to Stalin and his political personality. Materials are presented in four sections: "The Pursuit of Power," "The Role of the Party," "Instruments of Rule," and "Controls and Terrorism." Some reviewers prefer the first edition published in 1953.

B. STALINISM

B17. Geller, Mikhail, and Aleksandr Nekrich. *Utopia in Power: The History of the Soviet Union from 1917 to the Present.* New York: Summit Books, 1986, 877 p., bibliography.

The authors claim that Stalin represented the logical and perhaps inevitable heir to Lenin by continuing the latter's sacramental policy of fusing theory with terror, and also cite this policy to make a parallel case with Nazism. Geller and Nekrich do not feel that Trotsky would have done more for Russia, and they argue that Stalin dreaded a possible communist takeover in Germany in the 1920s because the U.S.S.R. would have appeared backward by comparison. Nekrich won some notoriety within Russia in the mid-1960s for his book *June 22, 1941*, which blamed Russia's early defeats in World War II on the alleged dereliction and carelessness of Stalin. Geller and Nekrich believe that Lenin, Stalin, and their system did not have a particularly Russian origin, and that, indeed, similarly repressive utopias have arisen throughout history in many other countries.

B18. Gill, Graeme J. *Stalinism.* Atlantic Highlands, NJ: Humanities Press International, 1990, 83 p., bibliography.

One of a series that presents scholarly summations of important areas of European history, this title concentrates on the multipart system crafted by Stalin and built in depth by his followers. Gill believes that much of the economic structure of Stalinism survived well into the 1980s, even though political and other aspects of the machine had been partially or largely dismantled. The author views Stalinism as both radical and reactionary, but does not see it as an inevitable outcome of its revolutionary roots. The text provides a brief survey of other research and arguments while making its own points.

B19. Khrushchev, Nikita S. *The Anatomy of Terror: Khrushchev's Revelations About Stalin's Regime.* Westport, CT: Greenwood Press, 1979, 73 p.

A recent reprint version of the author's famous 1956 secret speech to the 20th Congress of the C.P.S.U. in which he first "publicly" described and castigated the abuses by Stalin and the Cult of Personality. The actual text of the speech takes about 30-35 pages in this and other editions. Different people have contributed essays or annotations for variant editions. These have appeared under such titles as *The Crimes of the Stalin Era* (Annotated by Boris Nicolaevsky: New Leader, 1962), *The Secret Speech* (Introduced by the Medvedev brothers: Spokesman Books, 1976), *The Dethronement of Stalin,* and *The Truth About Stalin.* The Judiciary Committee of the U.S. Senate also published a G.P.O. copy in 1957 under the title *Speech of Nikita Khrushchev...*

B20. Kolarz, Walter. *Stalin and Eternal Russia.* London: Lindsay Drummond, 1991, 144 p., bibliography.

Kolarz urges his readers to view the Soviet Union in the context of its long history as much (or more) than in relation to its recent communist domination. He argues that Stalin chose to build Marxism in one country made up of many European and Asian peoples, whereas Trotsky wanted to pursue world revolution (p. 21, 1944 ed.). The author believes that Stalin actually created or magnified Soviet patriotism by tapping into the ancient Russian and Asian suspicion of Europe and the West. He also makes the point that many of the Soviet populace—especially those of Asian descent—have almost a psychological need for autocracy. First published in 1944.

B21. Labin, Suzanne. *Stalin's Russia.* London: Victor Gollancz, 1949, 492 p., bibliography.

Stalin's Russia describes and indicts the Stalinist system, spending some fifty pages focussing specifically on its leader. The seventeen chapters cover such topics as: the constitution, the secret police, the Red Army, propaganda, women's status, education, and foreign policy. Labin refers to the Soviet structure as the "resurrection of Pharaoism" (p. 105), and tries to utilize many Soviet documents as their own damning self-evidence. This translation of the original French-language text, *Staline le Terrible*, includes a new foreword by the noted writer and former communist, Arthur Koestler.

B22. **Lampert, Nicholas, and Gabor T. Rittersporn, eds.** *Stalinism: Its Nature and Aftermath: Essays in Honor of Moshe Lewin.* Armonk, NY: M. E. Sharpe, 1992, 291 p., bibliography.

This anthology of essays by scholars from the United States, Europe, and Great Britain covers many aspects of Stalinism, including its social, political and historiographic problems. *Stalinism* provides a useful overview of its subject, with most material suitable for the advanced reader.

B23. **Laqueur, Walter.** *The Fate of the Revolution: Interpretations of Soviet History from 1917 to the Present.* Rev. and updated ed. New York: Collier Books, 1987, 285 p., bibliography.

Laqueur's general study of the historiography of the Russian Revolution and Soviet history through the 1960s includes one chapter of particular interest to the student of the dictator. "Stalin: For and Against" analyzes the published biographies of Stalin. There is also other material on the Russian leader scattered throughout the book.

B24. **Lynch, Michael.** *Stalin and Khrushchev: The U.S.S.R., 1924-64.* London: Hodder & Stoughton, 1990, 138 p., bibliography.

In comparing the two Soviet leaders, the author claims that neither really succeeded in completely rejuvenating the Soviet economy. Lynch also feels that Stalin bequeathed a deep mistrust of change and of the outside world to his people. Stalin's economic and foreign policies are said to have come from his obsession to build up the U.S.S.R. and protect her from a legion of enemies. The horrendous extent of the purges, according to Lynch, may have derived from a combination of Stalin's paranoia and an almost anarchistic frenzy by middle- and low-level officials.

B25. **Lyons, Eugene.** *Assignment in Utopia.* New York: Harcourt, Brace & Co., 1937, 658 p.

This scathing denunciation of the Soviet form of socialism was penned by an American journalist for United Press International who had previously represented Tass in the U.S. before spending 1927-34 in Moscow. Although he strongly condemned the Stalinist system for its corrupt bureaucratization, its deceitful stage management of forced progress, and its barbaric and even fascistic injustice, Lyons remained somewhat charmed by the allegedly kind, unaffected personality of Stalin. Includes accounts of early and relatively unpublicized show trials that may have foreshadowed the big purges of the middle to late 1930s. A contemporary example of harsh disillusionment from a Westerner who had gone to Russia ready to sing the Soviet praises.

B26. **McNeal, Robert Hatch.** *The Bolshevik Tradition: Lenin, Stalin, Khrushchev, Brezhnev.* 2nd ed. Englewood Cliffs, NJ: Prentice-Hall, 1975, 210 p., bibliography.

McNeal places Stalin within a continuing line of semi-mythical Russian dictators, as part of a system originally designed by Vladimir Lenin for the ongoing governance of the Soviet Union.

B27. **Medvedev, Roy Aleksandrovich.** *Let History Judge: The Origins and Consequences of Stalinism.* Rev. ed. New York: Columbia University Press, 1989, 903 p.

Perhaps the capstone to Medvedev's many writings on Stalin, this book alleges that Stalinism arose from rational decisions by its namesake rather than from any mental delusions. Some readers may think the truth actually blends a mixture of pragmatism and paranoia. Medvedev here presents a massive tome of stories, statistics, and opinions on Stalin's rise, on his dedication to political terror, and on the terrible results of his social reconstruction. The author does not defend Lenin as he did in his earlier works, but does claim that Stalin received some popular support from a gullible Russian public.

B28. **Medvedev, Roy Aleksandrovich.** *On Stalin and Stalinism.* Oxford: Oxford University Press, 1979, 205 p.

Medvedev describes Stalin as a purely political animal and Stalinism as a beast that would devour true communism. The author tends to excuse Lenin from any accountability for the origins of official Soviet terror. Written from the viewpoint of one who wanted to believe in the viability of democratic communism, *On Stalin and Stalinism* concludes that Stalinism was anti-Leninist and that Stalin's negatives outweighed his positives. The title is a sequel to the original edition of *Let History Judge*; Medvedev revised his opinion of Lenin's influence in the revised version of the latter work.

B29. **Nove, Alec.** *Stalinism and After: The Road to Gorbachev.* 3rd ed. London & Boston: Unwin Hyman, 1989, 212 p., bibliography.

Rather than describe any psychological permutations, Nove prefers explanations that give Stalin and Stalinism the common trait of raw political instinct. Thus, we see the elimination of many intellectuals and their replacement by a generally ill-educated army of little Stalins.

The system thereby created lived on for many years following the death of its founder. By the close of this third edition, Nove portrays Gorbachev as admitting that Stalin's bloodbath techniques were wrong while arguing that fundamentals such as collectivization were correct. The original 1975 edition received mixed reviews. Some found the book did not reveal anything new, while others thought it avoided a capitalist slant and provided a useful outline. First published as *Stalinism and After*.

B30. **Petersen, Arnold.** *Stalinist Corruption of Marxism: A Study in Machiavellian Duplicity.* New York: New York Labor News, 1953, 156 p.

An update of the 1940 original edition by a well-known American Marxist, this title exploits a rich pamphleteering style to emotionally skewer Stalinism and its founder. Petersen portrays Stalin as a shoddy theorist and a devious manipulator who sometimes made clumsy mistakes while betraying the true Marxist cause.

B31. **Proskurin, Alexander, ed.** *The Stalin Phenomenon.* New Delhi, India: Sterling Publishers, 1989, 147 p.

A group of glasnost essays, letters, and interviews involving a variety of Soviet historians, journalists, and scholars (including Roy Medvedev). The pieces concentrate on political, social, economic, and military aspects of the Stalinist era. The general line throughout this book criticizes Stalin's tyrannical methods without making them an inevitable result of properly administered Marxism. The title essay—by Dmitry Volkogonoff—maintains that Lenin had even begun to build "democratic potential" (p. 112) into the system.

B32. **Randall, Francis B.** *Stalin's Russia: An Historical Reconsideration.* New York: Free Press, 1965, 328 p., bibliography.

This book is a general survey and analysis of the Soviet Union with a good amount of material on Stalin. Randall concludes that Stalin's personality was dominated by paranoia and megalomania that seriously affected his decisions in all areas. The evolution of Stalin's decisions is traced from his early revolutionary experiences in Georgia to his gaining dictatorial power in the 1930s. This book does not dwell on biographical particulars as much as other titles do. Rather, the author uses psychological and sociological theories to show how Stalin's character development led to his construction of a repressive, perhaps self-deluding system of government. Also among the topics covered are chapters on terror, propaganda, the bureaucracy, and industrialization. While Randall clearly believes Stalin did much more harm than good, he does credit him for making the Soviet Union a major military power, and for industrializing the country.

B33. Reiman, Michal. *The Birth of Stalinism: The USSR on the Eve of the "Second Revolution."* Bloomington: Indiana University Press, 1987, 188 p., bibliography.

A Czech historian, Reiman traces the development of Stalinism from its Leninist roots through the 1920s. The book is strongest in relating economics and social conditions to Stalin's policies and the way in which various elements of Soviet society all helped mold Stalin's new order. Reiman believes, however, that it was the force of Stalin's personality more than ideology that was the basis of Stalinism.

B34. Rigby, Thomas Henry, ed. *The Stalin Dictatorship: Khrushchev's "Secret Speech" and Other Documents.* University Park, PA: Pennsylvania State University Press, 1968, 128 p., bibliography.

The editor gives a long introduction to the Secret Speech, and provides three main reactions to Khrushchev's official revelations: (1) Many communists felt that the "core" (p. 18) of their political system had been shaken, since Stalin had built up so much of the ideological apparatus, (2) The Cult-of-Personality explanation did not really explain the deep extent of the rot, and, (3) The Soviet Union inevitably lost its monopoly role as the sole heartland of socialism. This title also includes extracts from a 1961 report by Khrushchev to the 22nd Congress and from the memoirs of a former People's Commissar for Armaments, B. L. Vannikov. The latter contends that Stalin's system bred both cruelty and inefficiency.

B35. Solzhenitsyn, Aleksandr. *The Gulag Archipelago, 1918-1956: An Experiment in Literary Investigation.* New York: Harper & Row, 1974-78, 3 vols., bibliography.

This work is a passionate and powerful criticism of the Soviet labor camp system created under Lenin, and greatly expanded by Stalin, who used it to silence his political critics. The account is partly autobiographical, but also relates the experiences of hundreds of other prisoners. Stalin is the focus directly or indirectly of much of this work, since the Gulag was an integral part of the Soviet system. Solzhenitsyn portrays Stalin in a somewhat cardboard manner; but, as with many titles concentrating on Soviet repression, *Gulag* does bring alive more than enough horror and irrationality in the system to reflect badly on its master. Unlike some other writers, however, Solzhenitsyn also gives considerable blame for the organized terror to both Lenin and the Czarist government. Some critics have been critical of the passionate nature of the work and of some inaccuracies of fact. Nonetheless, *The Gulag Archipelago* remains one of the most important works about the Stalinist era.

B36. *Stalin, for and Against: Soviet People on Stalinism and Its Consequences.* Moscow: Novosti Press, 1990, 79 p.

This book is an anthology of letters—or extracts of letters—to Soviet periodicals written by Soviets from different walks of life and different generations. Some of the writers defend Stalin, but the majority blame him for crimes against the Soviet people and for corrupting the true socialism of Lenin. Quotes are attributed to particular people but without any bibliographical references.

B37. **Strong, John W., ed.** *Essays on Revolutionary Culture and Stalinism: Selected Papers from the Third World Congress for Soviet and East European Studies.* Columbus, OH: Slavica Publishers, 1990, 244 p., bibliography.

These selected papers cover a range of specialized topics, many of which are specifically about Stalinism. Examples of several papers include: "The Russian Revolution and Stalinism: A Political Problem and Its Historiographic Content," "Party Opposition to Stalin (1930-1932) and the First Moscow Trial," and "Stalinism as a System of Communication." For the advanced student.

B38. **Timasheff, Nicholas.** *The Great Retreat: The Growth and Decline of Communism in Russia.* New York: E. P. Dutton, 1946, 470 p., bibliography.

A post-war analysis of the Soviet Union's drift away from the original ideals of communism. The cause, of course, is Stalin and the system he created. Although dated in part, much of the analysis is still valid. Written from the perspective of a sociologist.

B39. **Tolstoy, Nikolai.** *Stalin's Secret War.* New York: Holt, Rinehart, and Winston, 1982, 463 p.

Tolstoy, a cousin of noted novelist Leo Tolstoy, describes the abuses and horror of the Soviet system of government as indications of Stalin's compulsion to punish and isolate his people. The reader must decide whether he believes that the machinery of terror actually operated more secretly in relation to Western outsiders than to all the actual, ongoing, and potential victims living within the U.S.S.R. The author does not evaluate all of his sources well, a somewhat common failing or inevitable circumstance when trying to investigate a closed society and its secretive leader. He does claim, however, that Stalin was ready to roll the Red Army into Western Europe but that his death intervened. Pictures the Russian pattern of governance as perfidious yet clumsy.

B40. Tsipko, Aleksandr S. *Is Stalinism Really Dead?* New York: Harper & Row, 1990, 278 p.

An unfond farewell to the propaganda legends of Stalinism and even Marxism. The author worked in a state economics institute and utilized Gorbachev's relaxation of controls to debunk such ideas as the grassroots origin of the Personality Cult. Tsipko deprecates Stalin's system for its suppression of individuality, and also criticizes the works of Marx and Engels for allowing the dictator's wholesale coercion of his own people.

B41. Tucker, Robert C. *The Metamorphosis of the Stalin Myth*. Santa Monica, CA: Rand Corporation, 1954, 37 leaves.

Written during the interim between Stalin's death and Khrushchev's secret 1956 speech condemning much of Stalinism, this report analyzes early changes in Soviet political policy and the new official party view of the former dictator. Tucker describes the new oligarchy as trying to remold Stalin's image into one of a faithful, lifelong follower of Lenin and a strong proponent of collective leadership. In order perhaps to maintain communist control over the military, the new leaders did continue the legend or interpretation of Stalin as a strong wartime chief. This title represents an early "think-tank" publication of an author who would later produce many more publications concerning the Soviet Union.

B42. Tucker, Robert C. *Political Culture and Leadership in Soviet Russia: From Lenin to Gorbachev*. New York: W. W. Norton & Co., 1987, 214 p., bibliography.

Something of an update to the author's *The Soviet Political Mind*, this book continues the idea that Stalin acted as an extreme top-down revolutionary trying to replace most political and cultural elements of the pre-Revolution with an even stronger socialism than envisioned by Lenin and other founding Bolsheviks. Some may feel that Stalin's socialistic apparatus was not exactly pure in its theoretical heart.

B43. Tucker, Robert C. *The Soviet Political Mind: Stalinism and Post-Stalin Change.* Rev. ed. New York: W. W. Norton & Co., 1971, 304 p., bibliography.

A collection of ten of Tucker's essays evaluating different aspects of Stalin's influence over Soviet history and politics. One of the author's main conclusions is that the totalitarian state was created by Stalin and Stalinism and not Bolshevism or Leninism. Different historians may contend instead that much Russian history—modern and Czarist—demonstrates rather strong authoritarian fundamentals. Nevertheless, Tucker's effort stands as an excellent analysis of the era by a noted historian.

B44. Tucker, Robert C., ed. *Stalinism: Essays in Historical Interpretation.* New York: W. W. Norton & Co., 1977, 332 p., bibliography.

Tucker edited this anthology of papers presented at a conference on "Stalinism and Communist Political Culture" held at Bellagio, Italy, in 1975. Typical examples of the selections include: "Bolshevism and Stalinism," "Stalinism as Revolution from Above," and "Marxist Roots of Stalinism." An excellent collection with contributions from many leading scholars. Primarily for the advanced student.

B45. Urban, G. R., ed. *Stalinism: Its Impact on Russia and the World.* Cambridge, MA: Harvard University Press, 1986, 454 p.

Urban collects twenty dialogues and interviews with historians and former diplomats and officials, including: W. Averell Harriman, Adam Ulam, Robert Tucker, Milovan Djilas, and George Kennan. These contributors and the balance of "guests" from this selection of Radio Free Europe/Radio Liberty broadcasts spent many years researching, dealing with, and/or suffering under Stalin and Stalinism. Examples of the materials include: "Stalin Closely Observed" (Brazhanov), "Stalin at War" (Harriman), and "A Choice of Lenins?" (Tucker).

B46. Von Laue, Theodore H. *Why Lenin? Why Stalin? A Reappraisal of the Russian Revolution, 1900-1930.* 2nd ed. Philadelphia: J. B. Lippincott, 1971, 227 p., bibliography.

Von Laue explains the policies and actions of Lenin and Stalin as a possibly inevitable result of Russian backwardness. The harshness of Bolshevik programs is seen as the only method open to its leaders, and the author claims that Stalin wanted to industrialize his country to the point where he could destroy the sneering enemies of the West. The author's thesis would appear to rest upon the alleged Russian complexes of inferiority and superiority that predate the 1917 Revolution by many hundred years.

B47. Wolfe, Bertram David, ed. *Khrushchev and Stalin's Ghost: Text, Background, and Meaning of Khrushchev's Secret Report to the Twentieth Congress on the Night of February 24-25, 1956.* Westport, CT: Greenwood Press, 1983, 322 p.

A reprint of the classic 1956 denunciation speech by Khrushchev along with a biting commentary by Wolfe. The author also provides over 80 pages of background on events since Stalin's death and more than 50 pages of appendices with various documents. Khrushchev does not emerge as a warm-hearted liberator.

B48. **Wood, Alan.** *Stalin and Stalinism.* New York: Routledge, 1990, 68 p., bibliography.

This short study provides a succinct, scholarly overview of Stalin and Stalinism and their place in Soviet history. A "Chronological Chart" and "Glossary of Russian Technical Terms and Abbreviations" provide useful information for the beginning student. Highly recommended for a quick overview of the subject.

IDEOLOGY AND DOMESTIC POLITICS

B49. **Avtorkhanov, Abdurakhman.** *Stalin and the Soviet Communist Party: A Study in the Technology of Power.* New York: Praeger Publishers, 1983, 379 p., bibliography.

Avtorkhanov looks at the extreme measures used to transform the C.P.S.U. into a reflection of Stalin's driven personality. While centered around activities of 1928-38, the book also strongly implies a direct Stalinist connection with Lenin's death (poison is the supposed agent). However, the author did not reach the higher party strata before his N.K.V.D. arrest; thus, some caution is needed when reading this work due to the possible blurring of fact and fiction. This can be seen through such devices as questionable verbatim conversations. Nevertheless, the title provides good insights into Stalin and other party leaders. First appeared about 1959.

B50. **Bender, Frederic L.,** ed. *The Betrayal of Marx.* New York: Harper & Row, 1979, 452 p., bibliography.

This anthology presents selections of Engels, Luxemburg, Lenin, Trotsky, Bukharin, Stalin himself, and others to argue that the proletarian revolution was severely undermined by the autocratic excesses of Stalin. The editor believes that Lenin somewhat unwittingly prepared the way for his successor's crimes by encouraging the power monopoly of the C.P.S.U.

B51. Brzezinski, Zbigniew K. *The Permanent Purge: Politics in Soviet Totalitarianism.* Cambridge, MA: Harvard University Press, 1956, 256 p., bibliography.

Postulates the idea that Stalinist executions of party, government, and military leaders and followers actually served positive purposes such as cleaning out the dead wood, siphoning off political pressures, and catalyzing new methods. The Purge then may be seen as a necessary process of control and an inevitable result of totalitarian suspicion. Stalin is credited or debited with the responsibility for greatly regularizing terror as an enduring feature of Soviet management. Some critics did not feel the writer factored enough human distress into his equation. Brzezinski later served as a primary national security adviser to U.S. President Jimmy Carter.

B52. Cohen, Stephen F. *Bukharin and the Bolshevik Revolution: A Political Biography, 1888-1938.* New York: Alfred A. Knopf, 1973, 495 p., bibliography.

Cohen's book is the standard biography of Bukharin and an important work for gaining an understanding of the political undercurrents and political climate of Stalin's reign. Cohen is especially strong in showing how the terror of the 1930s developed. Stalin saw Bukharin as a threat to his own power, and sought first to discredit him and then to subject him to a phony trial and ultimately to a death sentence.

B53. Conquest, Robert. *Inside Stalin's Secret Police: N.K.V.D. Politics, 1936-1939.* Stanford, CA: Hoover Institution Press, 1985, 222 p., bibliography.

Conquest describes the chilling methods of the Soviet machine of sociopolitical terror, and maintains that raw brutality was the order of the day in general preference to any sophisticated, psychological means. The author places Stalin squarely at the center of the system in terms of both final responsibility and specific knowledge. Some estimates of the final carnage have reached twenty million, and Conquest shows how the Soviet leader arranged a rolling system of terror that crushed blameless citizens and then its own engineers.

B54. Daniels, Robert Vincent. *The Conscience of the Revolution: Communist Opposition in Soviet Russia.* Cambridge, MA: Harvard University Press, 1960, 526 p., bibliography.

Daniels has written "...a history of the differences within the Communist movement in Russia, and of all the groups that disputed with the movement's leaders."—Preface. Stalin was a prominent figure in many of these activities, and he later used these differences for his own purposes in the purges of the 1930s. Examples of subjects covered include: "The United Opposition," "The Right Opposition," and "Why the Opposition Failed." Appendix B, "Composition of the Chief Party Organs," is useful for its lists of members which are difficult to locate. This is a standard work on the subject.

B55. Daniels, Robert Vincent, ed. *A Documentary History of Communism in Russia.* Rev. ed. Hanover, VT: University Press of New England for the University of Vermont, 1984, 2 vols., bibliography.

The editor has selected some seventy documents and extracts for the 1922-1953 sections of this work, including items both supportive and critical of Stalin. A number of pieces were written by the dictator himself. Some of the latter mention such matters as the kulaks, the double-dealers and Trotskyites, dialectical materialism, and Marxist linguistics. Undermining contributors include Bukharin and Trotsky. Daniels gives brief, evaluative introductions to each section and selection, and tries to illustrate through the selections how Soviet Communism moved from a supposed classless liberation to a highly stratified and centralized machine of control.

B56. Fainsod, Merle. *Smolensk Under Soviet Rule.* Cambridge, MA: Harvard University Press, 1958, 484 p., bibliography.

Fainsod presents a local and regional picture of Soviet government during the years 1917-1938 when Stalin rose from regional to national power and then mercilessly consolidated his hold at all levels. The author built and documented this book through the use of a valuable cache of Communist Party sources seized by the Germans after their 1941 conquest of the Russian city of Smolensk. Further evidence from Moscow Center was not available to the invaders; however, the author has given us an important look at the local nature and effects of early and middle-aged Stalinism.

B57. Gill, Graeme J. *The Origins of the Stalinist Political System.* New York: Cambridge University Press, 1990, 454 p., bibliography.

While conceding that Stalinism had Leninist roots, the author argues that it developed into an extreme hybrid with heavy reliance on the "patrimonial model of power" (p. 327). Although Gill gives Stalin credit for emphasizing personality over institutions, he believes that the system really gained vital momentum of its own by creating the need for many small dictators at the sub-national levels. After all, Moscow could not keep an eye on every area. The collectivization of farms and the widespread political purges are viewed as economic, social, and political policies instigated by Stalin, but actually implemented and vitally supported by many underlings who thought they—and perhaps their country—would ultimately benefit. Indeed, the uprooting or destruction of millions of lives did create much job turnover and competition for new kinds of command replacements. The reader might ask, however, if the Stalinist model here propounded could have continued without acquiescence from Stalin himself. Compare with Dunmore [item B70].

B58. **Inkeles, Alex.** *Social Change in Soviet Russia.* Cambridge, MA: Harvard University Press, 1968, 475 p., bibliography.

This collection of articles represents twenty years of studies, and, although superseded in part, still remains relevant and its interpretations valid. Materials are presented in seven sections and cover such subjects as: "Social Groupings," "Public Opinion," and "Propaganda." A good overview of a number of specialized topics related to the social impact of Stalinism.

B59. **McCagg, William O.** *Stalin Embattled, 1943-1948.* Detroit: Wayne State University Press, 1978, 423 p., bibliography.

McCagg argues that Stalin's foreign policies would have seemed less aggressive had he not been strongly pushed by ideological zealots at home and abroad. The author portrays the dictator as a rational and practical man trying more to stay in control than to advance the communist cause. Some reviewers felt that McCagg's authentication did not match his interpretation, and they cite Russian involvement with the Korean War as one such contradiction.

B60. **McNeal, Robert Hatch**, ed. *Resolutions and Decisions of the Communist Party of the Soviet Union, Volume 3: The Stalin Years, 1929-1953.* Toronto: University of Toronto Press, 1974, 289 p., bibliography.

McNeal provided specific editing for this volume and general editing for the series, which had reached four volumes by 1974, intended to cover the period 1898-1964. These books may be regarded as shadow versions of the official Soviet set, and they give a Western perspective in their various general and specific introductions and notes. The series excludes other important documents, such as speeches by leaders, reports of the Central Committee, decisions by the Politburo, and many foreign policy matters. Even when further discounting the Stalin volume due to the reduction of official party meetings, however, one can find here many documents of interest: *e.g.*, a title discussing the tremendous triumphs of collectivization as well as the villainy of its inside "subverters," and another item on the terrorist acts of the Trotskyite-Zinovievite "wreckers."

B61. **Mehnert, Klaus.** *Stalin Versus Marx: The Stalinist Historical Doctrine.* Port Washington, NY: Kennikat Press, 1972, 128 p.

This book summarizes Soviet historiography's change from a Marxist to a Stalinist character. The new philosophy emphasized Russia's ancient primacy as a nation as well as focusing on the personality of its leaders. Both of these concepts would firmly underpin Stalin's need to tap into Russian patriotism during the struggle with Germany as well as his drive to build a highly personalized dictatorship. Translated and reprinted from the 1952 German original.

B62. **Merridale, Catherine.** *Moscow Politics and the Rise of Stalin: The Communist Party in the Capital, 1925-32.* New York: St. Martin's Press, 1990, 328 p., bibliography.

Merridale emphasizes Communist Party history, but he also includes material on the effect of Stalin's rise to power, and a comparison of changes in party structure and attitudes in the 1920s and 1930s as Stalin gained more and more authority.

B63. **Rittersporn, Gabor Tamas.** *Stalinist Simplifications and Soviet Complications: Social Tensions and Political Conflicts in the USSR, 1933-1953.* New York: Harwood Academic Publishers, 1991, 334 p., bibliography.

Rittersporn takes the position that Stalin did not control events to the extent generally accepted, but was himself controlled by the bureaucracy. There is a detailed discussion of the "Great Terror" or "Yezhovshchina" ("Yezhov Times," so named for N.K.V.D. chief Yezhov), and Stalin's role in these events. The author contends that Stalin was not solely responsible for the terror, but rather that it was carried forward by an uncontrollable bureaucracy with its own goals. Rittersporn also argues that the "chaos" created by the terror actually weakened Stalin's ability to control events.

B64. Rosenfeldt, Niels Erik. *Knowledge and Power: The Role of Stalin's Secret Chancellery in the Soviet System of Government.* Copenhagen: Rosenkilde and Bagger, 1978, 219 p., bibliography.

A specialized study of the secret bureaucratic structure which operated outside the usual government bureaus, gathering information for Stalin and assisting in seeing that his decisions were implemented. The author provides a detailed analysis of the structure and role of the chancellery. Three of the better known heads of the "Secret Department" were Ivan Tovstukha, Lev Mekhlis, and Alexander Poskrebyshev (who served Stalin for twenty-five years). The "Secret Chancellery" played a crucial role in Stalin's development of the powerful political base on which he built his dictatorship.

B65. Rosenfeldt, Niels Erik. *Stalin's Special Departments: A Comparative Analysis of Key Sources.* Copenhagen: University of Copenhagen, Institute of Slavonic and East European Studies, 1989, 116 p., bibliography.

This continuation of the author's earlier study, *Knowledge and Power* [item B64], provides an analysis of "Stalin's power apparat," the Special Section of the Communist Party Central Committee which Stalin used to build a political base. A specialized study of interest primarily to the advanced student.

B66. **Salisbury, Harrison E.** *Moscow Journal: The End of Stalin.* Chicago: University of Chicago Press, 1975, 449 p.

Written in a form that combines sample dispatches with ongoing commentary, Salisbury's effort reveals the ultra-controlled, paranoid system he experienced in Moscow towards the end of Stalin's life. Another work that perhaps describes the Man of Steel more through his effects on Soviet society than through normal biographical forms. Originally published in 1961.

B67. **Tucker, Robert C.** *The Politics of Soviet De-Stalinization.* Santa Monica, CA: Rand Corporation, 1957, 54 leaves.

Tucker contends that Stalin went beyond a primary stage of organizing totalitarianism, and actually destroyed the original Communist Party system by setting up a complete dictatorship (p. ii). Following the Second World War, Stalin's autocratic system could only survive by continuing its conservative, extremely hierarchical command. De-Stalinization after 1953 did not—to Tucker—mean official dismantling of the basic central control of the Soviet state and its economy, only a move away from Personality-Cult politics.

ECONOMICS AND INDUSTRIALIZATION

B68. **Bergson, Abram.** *The Real National Income of Soviet Russia Since 1928.* Cambridge, MA: Harvard University Press, 1961, 472 p., bibliography.

This book is "...an attempt to calculate for the period 1928-1955 the 'real' national income of the Soviet Union"—Introduction. Detailed, scholarly, and definitive, Bergson's book is not easy reading, but provides a good overview of the effect of Stalinist policy on Soviet economic development.

B69. Boettke, Peter J. *The Political Economy of Soviet Socialism: The Formative Years, 1918-1928.* Boston: Kluwer Academic, 1990, 246 p., bibliography.

This "...systematic treatise on economic theory...discusses the central problems of political economy..." of the Soviet Union. Stalin, of course, was involved in the development of many of these early policies. While the book focuses primarily on the Russian economy, Stalin is mentioned throughout.

B70. Dunmore, Timothy. *The Stalinist Command Economy: The Soviet State Apparatus and Economic Policy, 1945-53.* New York: St. Martin's Press, 1980, 176 p., bibliography.

Dunmore presents the idea that Soviet economic policies in the post-war years moved away from complete, central control as bureaucratic momentum—or the lack thereof—began to overpower Stalin's dwindling capabilities. Compare with Gill's *The Origins of the Stalinist Political System* [item B57].

B71. Hughes, James. *Stalin, Siberia, and the Crisis of the New Economic Policy.* Cambridge, England: Cambridge University Press, 1991, 260 p., bibliography.

Hughes theorizes that Stalin's 1928 trip to Siberia persuaded the dictator to largely abandon Lenin's New Economic Policy (NEP) of temporarily conciliating the peasants. Instead, the Soviet government decided to accelerate a program to force collectivization of the farms and to wipe out the kulak class of petty landowners. Given that the Siberian visit may have been Stalin's last journey to any agricultural area, and given the unusual strength of farming and kulaks in the region, the reader might conclude that Stalin modelled an important program on an anomalous situation. Many critics contend that Stalin seemingly made many decisions based on false evidence and that he really used such rationales as excuses for the

implementation of his own hidden agenda. In any case,
this title is valuable for showing the dictator in his relationship with regional officials and in pursuit of national
agricultural transformation.

B72. **Kuromiya, Hiroaki.** *Stalin's Industrial Revolution: Politics and Workers, 1928-1932.* Cambridge: Cambridge
University Press, 1990, 364 p., bibliography.

The author contends that the proletariat supported the vi-
olence of the First Five-Year Plan because it would supposedly remove the social class that was exploiting them.
Kuromiya assumes that Soviet workers would believe that
many of the "exploiters" had somehow survived in power
for more than a decade after the 1917 October Revolution. Another illustration of the sales/propaganda skills
of Stalin. Based on the author's Princeton doctoral
thesis.

B73. **Nove, Alex.** *An Economic History of the U.S.S.R.,
1917-1991.* 3rd ed. New York: Penguin, 1992, 473
p., bibliography.

An Economic History of the U.S.S.R. contains a lengthy
account of the early years of Stalin's rule, when he
shaped and strengthened his centralized command economy. Nove describes the industrial experimentation and
economic engineering that occurred under Stalinization,
and does not much ruminate on the questions of social
upheaval, morality, or possible alternative programs.

B74. **Zaleski, Eugene.** *Stalinist Planning for Growth, 1933-
1952.* Chapel Hill: University of North Carolina
Press, 1980, 788 p., bibliography.

This definitive study of economic planning during the
Stalin era shows that political and not economic reasons
were frequently the basis of major economic decisions
during the Stalinist period. Roughly one-third of the
book consists of statistical data relative to all aspects of

the Soviet economy. The book is important but not easy reading, with a lengthy bibliography of sources that will prove invaluable for the student of Soviet economics. A related pre-Stalin study by Zaleski is *Planning for Economic Growth in the Soviet Union, 1918-1932* (Chapel Hill: University of North Carolina Press, 1971).

CULTURE AND SOCIETY

B75. **Carrère d'Encausse, Hélène.** *Stalin: Order Through Terror.* New York: Longman, 1981, 269 p., bibliography.

The second of a two-volume series covering 1917-1953 in the Soviet Union, this work follows one on Lenin, and contends that the latter established at least some of the terroristic tools, if not much of the philosophical cant, employed by his successor. Agrarian, economic, and social revolutions are also described along with the state means of control. Carrère d'Encausse's well-received study concludes that Stalin's ability to carry out a social and economic revolution depended upon his understanding of how to acquire and use power.

B76. **Fitzpatrick, Sheila, ed.** *Cultural Revolution in Russia, 1928-1931.* Bloomington: Indiana University Press, 1978, 309 p., bibliography.

This anthology of academic papers focuses on the cultural changes, especially among the intelligentsia, during the time of the First Five-Year Plan. During this period the position of the intelligentsia, especially the non-communist sector, steadily advanced. Examples of topics covered include: "Cultural Revolution as Class War," "The Construction of the Stalinist Psyche," and "The Cultural Revolution and Western Understanding of the Soviet System." The editor's introduction gives background information and provides a unifying theme.

B77. Gunther, Hans, ed. *The Culture of the Stalin Period.* New York: St. Martin's Press, 1990, 291 p.

The Culture of the Stalin Period includes a selection of brief academic papers covering a wide range of cultural activities undertaken during Stalin's era. The essays attempt to find a common denominator in defining the type of culture created in an era of heavy political-social demands. The fifteen contributions are grouped into five general categories: "Popular Culture, Everyday Life, Ideology," "Art," "Literature," "Architecture," and "Film."

B78. Holmes, Larry E. *The Kremlin and the Schoolhouse: Reforming Education in Soviet Russia, 1917-1931.* Bloomington: Indiana University Press, 1991, 214 p., bibliography.

Holmes's book is of interest here because it contains certain materials on Stalin's influence over school reforms not readily found in other sources. Holmes maintains that, in spite of all of Stalin's efforts, Soviet schools did not become significant agents of major social change at least through 1931.

B79. Kopelev, Lev. *The Education of a True Believer.* New York: Harper & Row, 1980, 328 p.

A personal account of Kopelev's work in the Communist Party in the 1920s and '30s. Kopelev presents valuable insights into Soviet society and tells how he became a strong supporter of Stalin. The reader gets a good "feel" for the excitement of the times and the belief that the social and political structure of the Soviet state was being changed for the better. Kopelev later became a Soviet dissident and abandoned Stalinism. Two other volumes of memoirs with some additional material on Stalin are: *To Be Preserved Forever* (Philadelphia: Lippincott, 1977) and *Ease My Sorrows: A Memoir* (New York: Random House, 1983).

B80. **Kostiuk, Hryhory.** *Stalinist Rule in the Ukraine: A Study of the Decade of Mass Terror, 1929-1939.* New York: Praeger Publishers, 1961, 162 p., bibliography.

This account of the impact of Stalinist rule in the Ukraine is based primarily on excellent documentation and partly on the author's personal experiences in labor camps in the 1930s. Kostiuk shows the overwhelming effect of Soviet policies on all levels of society and on the economic and social structure. He also includes material on Khrushchev's responsibility for implementing Stalin's policies. The techniques developed for punishing the Ukrainians may have served as a horribly effective model for the tyrant's oppression of many other Soviet nationalities. Some reviewers thought Kostiuk's effort a bit *nouveau* propagandistic in its anti-Stalinism.

B81. **Kravchenko, Victor.** *I Chose Freedom: The Personal and Political Life of a Soviet Official.* New York: Charles Scribner's Sons, 1946, 496 p.

At the time of this book's publication, the U.S. and the U.S.S.R. had just concluded a four-year interlude of co-operation against the Axis powers and were resuming a bitter ideological struggle on a larger scale. Perhaps the relative wartime harmony made some of Kravchenko's reviewers suspicious of his strong denunciations of the Stalinist path, for these particular critics disagreed wildly with most others on the quality and veracity of this title. As with many works in the present bibliography, *I Chose Freedom* looks less at Stalin than at the paranoid and irrational society he wrought—perhaps in his own image.

B82. **Lewin, Moshe.** *The Making of the Soviet System: Essays in the Social History of Interwar Russia.* New York: Pantheon, 1985, 354 p., bibliography.

Lewin provides a comprehensive survey of urban and rural Soviet society as it developed in the 1920s and '30s, including an analysis of the relationship between the Soviet people and Communist Party politics. Especially useful for studying the background of the developing Stalinism. This work is most suitable for the advanced student.

B83. **Mandel'shtam, Nadezhda.** *Hope Against Hope: A Memoir.* New York: Atheneum, 1970, 431 p.

This enthusiastically received work is partly a memoir and partly a biography of Osip Mandel'shtam, the author's husband and a famous poet of the 1930s. Essentially, the work is about the confrontation between Stalin and Osip Mandel'shtam over his anti-Stalin poems. Osip was arrested, released, and rearrested, and eventually died in the purges of 1937-1938. An interesting and important view of Stalinist society in the 1930s. A recent collection of Osip Mandel'shtam's poems is: *The Eyesight of Wasps* (Columbus: Ohio State University Press, 1989).

B84. **Mikhailkov-Konchalovskii, Andrei Sergeevich, and Alexander Lipkov.** *The Inner Circle: An Inside View of Soviet Life Under Stalin.* New York: Newmarket Press, 1991, 147 p., bibliography.

This heavily illustrated summary of life at different levels of society during the reign of Stalin includes photographs said to have been newly-released from Soviet archives. The work covers the everyday experiences of Alexander Ganshin, the dictator's movie projectionist from 1935, as well as the social conditions for common folk not employed at the Kremlin. Interspersed throughout the text and photos are quotations from such writers as John Steinbeck, Svetlana Alliluyeva (Stalin's daughter), Nadezhda Mandel'stam, and Ilya Ehrenburg. Ganshin is portrayed as representing the millions of Russians who may have been mesmerized by a benign, paternal image of Stalin. These people could hardly believe that their leader was truly aware of the system's everyday atrocities. The book closes with a discussion of the creation of the film, *The Inner Circle*, which used Ganshin's life as a focus to comment on the effects of Stalinism.

B85. Miller, Frank J. *Folklore for Stalin: Russian Folklore and Pseudofolklore of the Stalin Era.* Armonk, NY: M. E. Sharpe, 1990, 192 p., bibliography.

The focus of this work is the folklore "...created by Russian folklorist and folk performers in the 1930s in order to propagandize official Communist party ideals among the masses"—Preface. Stalin, of course, was the subject of a good deal of this myth-making. The author gives many examples of folklore used to establish the "Stalin Cult." Miller also shows that much of the folklore claimed as authentic by Soviet scholars of the period was simulated. This is an interesting and informative study of the era that gives a unique perspective.

B86. Nove, Alec. *Glasnost in Action: Cultural Renaissance in Russia.* Boston: Unwin Hyman, 1989, 251 p., bibliography.

"This book represents an attempt to give to the nonspecialist reader some notion of what has happened in the Soviet cultural scene in recent years"—Preface. The issues of Stalin and Stalinism are discussed throughout the book. A great part of recent Soviet culture is concerned with coming to terms with its own past, as represented by the Stalin era. Examples of the subjects covered include: "Stalin and Stalinism," "The Rehabilitation of History—On the History of Rehabilitation," "The Terror," and "Politics, Sociology, and Law."

B87. Siniavskii, Andrei. *Soviet Civilization: A Cultural History.* New York: Arcade Publishing, Little, Brown & Co., 291 p.

Siniavskii, a Russian novelist in exile, has written a general popular survey of Soviet culture based primarily on an analysis of Soviet literature. While not the main subject of the book, Stalin is mentioned throughout the text. The author maintains that the communists created a new civilization that distorted Russian history and culture. Some of the topics covered include: "Stalin: The Church State," "Utopia Found," "The New Man," "The Soviet Way of Life," and "The Soviet Language."

ARTS AND HUMANITIES

B88. **Barber, John.** *Soviet Historians in Crisis, 1928-1932.* New York: Holmes & Meier, 1981, 194 p., bibliography.

This specialized study centers on the transformation of Soviet historiography during the first few years of Stalin's consolidation of power. Specifically, the chapter on "Stalin's Intervention" highlights the early impact that Stalin had on Soviet historians and their writings. This controlled intervention by the state apparatus into the shaping of contemporary and past Russian history was to continue for decades. *Soviet Historians in Crisis* is of interest as an example of Stalin's pervasive influence on nearly every intellectual endeavor. Not until glasnost were Russian writers once again allowed to conduct legitimate historical research—and to publish their findings.

B89. **Bown, Matthew Cullerne.** *Art Under Stalin.* New York: Holmes & Meier, 1991, 256 p., bibliography.

Bown's well-written book provides an excellent overview of Soviet art from the 1930s through the mid-1950s. An introductory chapter, "Art Under Lenin, 1917-24," discusses the early development of art under Bolshevik rule, a period which leads directly into the Stalinist era. Numerous illustrations of political and "Stalin Cult" art are presented, each accompanied by a brief penetrating analysis. Much of the material is based on conversations and interviews conducted by the author in the Soviet Union.

A final section, "Artists' Biographies," gives brief biographical sketches of each major artist.

B90. **Dunham, Vera Sandomirsky.** *In Stalin's Time: Middle-Class Values in Soviet Fiction.* Enlarged and updated ed. Durham, NC: Duke University Press, 1990, 288 p., bibliography.

First published in 1976, this study of Soviet fiction emphasizes the relationship of the Russian people to their government and to Stalinism as described in popular literature. A specialized work for the advanced student.

B91. **Golomstock, Igor.** *Totalitarian Art: In the Soviet Union, the Third Reich, Fascist Italy and The People's Republic of China.* New York: Icon Editions, 1990, 416 p., bibliography.

A general study of modern totalitarian art, with Stalin as one of the subjects. Golomstock shows how this art form develops in a given totalitarian system and how it serves the system. A specialized study with limited but interesting material on Stalin.

B92. **Kemp-Welch, Alice.** *Stalin and the Literary Intelligentsia, 1928-39.* New York: St. Martin's Press, 1991, 338 p., bibliography.

The primary emphasis of this study is Stalin's influence over writers in the period from his early gathering of power through the time of his fully developed dictatorship. Kemp-Welch covers in detail Stalin's influence on literature and his influence over the official Soviet literary organization, RAPP (Russian Association of Proletarian Writers). A specialized study useful to the advanced reader.

B93. **Marsh, Rosalind J.** *Images of Dictatorship: Portraits of Stalin in Literature.* New York: Routledge, 1989, 267 p., bibliography.

The central theme of this work is the treatment of Stalin in literature. Most of the writers covered are Russian—except for Koestler and Orwell—and most of the work is concerned with Rybakov's and Solzhenitsyn's novels. A well-written literary analysis mentioning most of the fictional works in which Stalin is a character.

B94. **Marsh, Rosalind J.** *Soviet Fiction Since Stalin: Science, Politics and Literature.* Rev. ed. Ann Arbor, MI: UMI Research Press, 1985, 152 p., bibliography.

This book is "...a political and historical study of the way in which one important subject—the theme of science and technology—has been treated in Soviet fiction in one period of Soviet history"—Introduction. Marsh uses "fiction as a documentary source" to study Soviet literature, which during this period was greatly affected by Stalin's policies. Of particular interest is the chapter, "The Effect of Stalinism on Science and Technology."

B95. **Struve, Gleb.** *Russian Literature Under Lenin and Stalin, 1917-1953.* Norman: University of Oklahoma Press, 1971, 454 p., bibliography.

Because the author excludes writers unpublished until after Stalin's death, this title basically surveys highly strictured literary output that could not stray very far from the party line without severe or fatal risks. Struve shows how Soviet literature as a whole moved from revolutionary idealism to socialist realism to national defense and finally to a kind of sterile mindlessness under the growing power of Stalinist cultural controls. Individual lights still shone out here and there for such genres as satire, but the best literature written during the period was probably left in hidden drawers.

B96. **Werth, Alexander.** *Musical Uproar in Moscow.* Westport, CT: Greenwood Press, 1973, 103 p.

Werth describes one of the more bizarre examples of how far Stalin would go in trying to transform Soviet culture. In this case, Andrei Zhdanov and other Party leaders in 1948 accused previously honored musicians such as Sergei Prokofiev and Dmitrii Shostakovich of displaying formalist, anti-revolutionary leanings in their work. The absurdity of these charges compares with Stalin's attacks on politically incorrect linguists or scientists.

SCIENCE AND TECHNOLOGY

B97. **Bailes, Kendall E.** *Technology and Society Under Lenin and Stalin: Origins of the Soviet Technical Intelligentsia, 1917-1941.* Princeton: Princeton University Press, 1978, 472 p., bibliography.

The focus of this study is the place of engineers and technicians in the Stalinist order from 1928-1941. The problems faced by this professional group are reflective of the issues and concerns of many professional classes. As more engineers came from the party and not from pre-revolutionary times, the status of the group grew and it eventually became an elite part of Soviet society. The book has good material on the origins of the purges, their effect on technicians and engineers, and the place of technology in Soviet society.

B98. **Joravsky, David.** *The Lysenko Affair.* Cambridge: Harvard University Press, 1970, 459 p., bibliography.

This is the standard work on an unusual episode in Soviet science. Trofim Lysenko was an uneducated peasant who was able to convince Soviet leaders—who for political reasons wanted to be persuaded—that his new agricultural methods would significantly increase crop yields. Of course, the harvests did not increase, and the science of genetics was destroyed for many years in the Soviet Union. This complex subject is carefully explained by Joravsky, and readers should have no problem understanding the technical materials. An important look at how Stalin's political priorities overrode established scientific methods.

B99. **Medvedev, Zhores A.** *The Rise and Fall of T. D. Lysenko.* New York: Columbia University Press, 1969, 284 p., bibliography.

Well-known commentator Medvedev chronicles how the Soviet government politicized and irrationalized biological research from 1929 through the early 1960s. Lysenko was Stalin's tool in this absurd fiasco in agricultural genetics, with the dictator himself touting his supposed abilities as a genetic theorist. Medvedev personally observed the warping of research priorities and the ability of scientists to conduct their experiments without interference, and he later helped to restore some balance to the system after Khrushchev's departure in 1964. The Lysenko affair synthesized all of the efforts by Stalin and his cronies to control thought in every field of intellectual endeavor.

C.

SPECIAL TOPICS

COLLECTIVIZATION OF AGRICULTURE

C1. **Conquest, Robert.** *The Harvest of Sorrow: Soviet Collectivization and the Terror-Famine.* New York: Oxford University Press, 1986, 412 p., bibliography.

Well-known political commentator Conquest has written the best and most thorough study to date of the 1932-1933 famine in the Ukraine and surrounding regions. The famine-terror was purposely created by Stalin to force the peasants onto collective farms, and to eliminate Ukrainian nationalism through the destruction of its churches, intelligentsia, and culture. Conquest estimates that millions died while the Soviet government refused to allow outside help into the area.

C2. **Lewin, Moshe.** *Russian Peasants and Soviet Power: A Study of Collectivization.* Evanston: Northwestern University Press, 1968, 539 p., bibliography.

Lewin, a noted scholar of the Soviet period, has written the standard work on the Soviet agricultural collectivization of the 1930s. His study covers the social, economic, and ideological elements of collectivization, and touches as well upon the turmoil and ultimate tragedy of the era. Central to the program was Stalin's deliberate policy to force the peasants into the collectives and state farms. This work is primarily for advanced students.

PURGES AND TERROR

C3.   **Carmichael, Joel.** *Stalin's Masterpiece: The Show Trials and Purges of the Thirties—The Consolidation of the Bolshevik Dictatorship.* New York: St. Martin's Press, 1976, 238 p., bibliography.

Carmichael argues that the Soviet dictator intricately crafted the entire absurd tragedy of the purges without losing any control of the process or giving way to any psychotic savagery. He describes the transformation of Bolshevism into a dualistic moral creed, with Stalin portrayed as the agent of virtue, and Trotsky and Bukharin as the archvillains of evil. Some historians have questioned Carmichael's thesis, believing that the violent, unchecked actions of such handpicked Stalinist tools as Yagoda and Beria indicate a lack of control at the helm of the Soviet state.

C4.   **Commission of Inquiry into the Charges Made Against Leon Trotsky in the Moscow Trials.** *Not Guilty: Report of the Commission.* New York: Monad Press, 1938, 422 p.

Some contemporary reviewers portrayed the Moscow trials and the purges as unfortunate squabbles detracting from the progress of a fascinating, socioeconomic experiment. Some also accepted the argument that Stalin needed to weed out internal opposition in order to strengthen the Soviet Union against the growing German and Japanese threats. Although the Commission that conducted this study included among its members such liberals as its chair, John Dewey, it still concluded that Stalin had thoroughly framed his old antagonist.

C5.   **Conquest, Robert.** *The Great Terror: A Reassessment.* New York: Macmillan, 1990, 570 p., bibliography.

This new study of the "Great Terror" of the mid-1930s is *not* a revision of Conquest's earlier work, *The Great Ter-*

ror: Stalin's Purge of the Thirties [item C6]. The most recently released samizdat writings and other documents now available under glasnost have been compared with the earlier documentation used by Conquest in the 1960s. The author concludes that the newest information merely confirms and reinforces the conclusions of his original study. This work presents a valuable modern reassessment of a critical period in Stalin's career.

C6.   **Conquest, Robert.** *The Great Terror: Stalin's Purge of the Thirties.* Rev. ed. New York: Macmillan, 1973, 844 p., bibliography.

This work is a comprehensive, fully documented history of the "Great Terror" of 1936 to 1938. The terror started with the murder of Kirov (likely planned by Stalin) and ended with a series of political trials that eliminated all of Stalin's perceived enemies and thousands of lesser party members. Conquest covers the historical background and the events of the terror and gives an analysis of the resulting changes in Soviet society and the Communist party. This work was first published in 1968. A later work by Conquest, *The Great Terror: A Reassessment* [item C5], is a follow-up to this work and uses the latest information coming out of the Soviet Union. For a different interpretation, see J. Arch Getty, *Origins of the Great Purges* [item C9].

C7.   **Conquest, Robert.** *Stalin and the Kirov Murder.* New York: Oxford University Press, 1989, 164 p., bibliography.

The author believes that Kirov's murder on December 1, 1934 was "the key moment which determined the development of the Soviet system..."—Introduction. The murder was used by Stalin as the justification for eliminating the "enemies of the state" during the Great Terror which followed. Conquest concludes—based upon circumstantial evidence—that Stalin planned the murder to eliminate a politician whose popularity was rapidly making him a potential rival. When he was killed, Kirov was head of the Leningrad party organization and a member of the Central Committee, and was seen by some as a possible successor to Stalin. An excellent book on an important, internal Soviet conspiracy.

C8. **Feuchtwanger, Lion.** *Moscow, 1937.* New York: Viking Press, 1937, 151 p.

Early observations on the purge trials from a somewhat pro-Stalin German novelist. The dictator is portrayed as a down-to-earth and even humorous leader. Some contemporary reviewers thought Feuchtwanger a bit naive.

C9. **Getty, J. Arch.** *Origins of the Great Purges: The Soviet Communist Party Reconsidered, 1933-1938.* New York: Cambridge University Press, 1985, 276 p., bibliography.

This controversial study maintains that the purges of the 1930s were not primarily Stalin's idea but originated from conflicts within the Communist party. Further, Getty believes that the Kirov murder was not part of a conspiracy by Stalin. For a contrasting interpretation of the origin of the purges, see Robert Conquest's *The Great Terror: Stalin's Purge of the Thirties* [item C6]. An important, provocative, and still controversial work.

C10. **Hodos, George H.** *Show Trials: Stalinist Purges in Eastern Europe, 1948-1954.* New York: Praeger Publishers, 1987, 193 p., bibliography.

The author describes how the East European countries were conquered by Russia during World War II, then suffered a cruel replay of the 1930s' Russian purges. Hodos feels this derived from Stalin's conflict with Tito as well as the need to fully subordinate all satellite lands through the Soviet model of terror. Many victims in Hungary and Czechoslovakia were Jews as well as devout Stalinists, and the author himself was a political prisoner in Hungary. As with many other sources of its kind, the Hodos title does not rely on full documentation, and hence is ultimately unprovable.

C11. **Levytsky, Borys, ed.** *The Stalinist Terror in the Thirties: Documentation from the Soviet Press.* Stanford, CA: Hoover Institution Press, 1974, 521 p., bibliography.

The documents in this anthology cover the Soviet "Terror" which began in 1936, with primary coverage of the three Moscow show trials. A lengthy introduction gives the historical background and explains the importance of the documents. Appendices list the more notable victims of these trials.

C12. **Orlov, Alexander.** *The Secret History of Stalin's Crimes.* New York: Random House, 1953, 366 p.

Orlov, a former N.K.V.D. operative who defected to the West, has written a survey of Stalinist terror and Stalin's personal involvement. The author emphasizes the three Moscow trials of 1936, 1937, and 1938. The roles of the secret police and other state agencies are discussed, based on the author's personal knowledge of the N.K.V.D., an advantage he often uses well. A number of personal anecdotes are included as well as reconstructed conversations. The book must be read with care, since the author was for some time part of the system he is exposing and condemning.

C13. **Tucker, Robert C., and Stephen F. Cohen, eds.** *The Great Purge Trial.* New York: Grosset & Dunlap, 1965, 725 p., bibliography.

A new reprinting of the 1938 book about the Moscow show trials. In his introduction, Tucker explores Stalin's suspicious megalomania as a purge motivator, and also contends that the dictator was somehow cleaning his house, perhaps to prepare for the coming Russo-German entente. Bukharin's statements may be seen as lonely warnings to later Marxists amidst a somewhat secretive cataclysm. Includes biographical data on a number of prominent victims.

C14. **Vaksberg, Arkady.** *The Prosecutor and the Prey: Vyshinsky and the 1930s' Moscow Show Trials.* London: Weidenfeld and Nicolson, 1990, 374 p.

Vaksberg tells the story of Stalin's chief prosecutor during the 1936-1938 purges, whose close but fearful relationship with the Soviet leader was central to the unfolding tragedy. The author shows in detail Vyshinsky's role in falsification of evidence, badgering of witnesses, and other outright illegalities to eliminate all possible political opposition to Stalin. Unlike such accessories of the scourge as Yagoda and Yezhov, Vyshinsky survived the trials and eventually served as Soviet Foreign Minister and as a permanent delegate to the United Nations. In spite of or because of his own fear, Vyshinsky played such dangerous games as routinely preparing position papers on opposite sides of the same question to utilize later with however his master's pronouncements actually fell. This book provides another view of the devious but servile nature of the political atmosphere surrounding Stalin. Also appeared in the United States as *Stalin's Prosecutor: The Life of Andrei Vyshinsky.*

MILITARY AFFAIRS AND THE GREAT PATRIOTIC WAR

C15. **Alexandrov, Victor.** *The Tukhachevsky Affair.* Englewood Cliffs, NJ: Prentice-Hall, 1964, 201 p., bibliography.

An unsubstantiated but fascinating account of the demise of one of Stalin's most brilliant young military leaders, a man who became a Soviet marshal in the mid-1930s but was subsequently arrested and executed. The dictator may have suspected that many of his more gifted generals

and officers represented a threat to his power; but, of
course, the widescale purge of the military hierarchy also
eliminated many who might later have succeeded in more
quickly defeating Nazi Germany. Alexandrov believes
that Stalin fabricated the conspiratorial documents that
implied Tukhachevsky actually worked for the Nazis.
The author uses a somewhat fictional style with the kinds
of detailed conversations one would find in a novel.

C16. **Bialer, Seweryn, ed.** *Stalin and His Generals: Soviet
Military Memoirs of World War II.* New York: Pega-
sus, 1969, 644 p., bibliography.

The compiler has selected parts of the memoirs of forty-
five Soviet military leaders for inclusion in this book.
The pieces are interesting for their insights into military
life before and during World War II, and for describing
the relations between the military leaders and Stalin.
Stalin is seen as a good wartime leader. The compiler's
introduction and notes are useful and provide unity to the
material.

C17A. **Erickson, John.** *The Road to Berlin: Continuing the
History of Stalin's War with Germany.* Boulder, CO:
Westview Press, 1983, 877 p., bibliography.
C17B. **Erickson, John.** *The Road to Stalingrad: Stalin's War
with Germany.* New York: Harper & Row, 1975, 594
p., bibliography.

These volumes are a standard military history of the So-
viet Union's war with Nazi Germany between 1941-1945.
The materials on Stalin include his pre-war purge of the
Soviet military hierarchy and his wartime role as a strate-
gist and military leader. An important evaluation of
Stalin as military leader.

C18. **Seaton, Albert.** *Stalin as Military Commander.* New
York: Praeger Publishers, 1976, 312 p., bibliography.

Seaton's book is unusual in devoting around 100 pages to Stalin's military leadership and style during the Revolution, while providing some of the same material and conclusions for the Great Patriotic War that may be found elsewhere. The command style of the Soviet ruler comes across as erratic but totally authoritarian. The English edition is entitled, *Stalin as Warlord.*

C19. **Shtemenko, S. M.** *The Soviet General Staff at War, 1917-1945.* Moscow: Progress Publishers, 1975-86, 2 vols.

Shtemenko chronicles the activities of the Red Army central staff during the struggle with Germany and provides both military and personal views of Stalin. The author claims that the Supreme Commander did not make major decisions strictly on his own. We also read about Stalin giving rather elaborate directions to frontline commanders as well as arranging daily work schedules and rest periods for General Headquarters staff. In addition, the volumes include such informal anecdotes as one that has the dictator regularly substituting ice water for vodka. Shtemenko held the rank of General of the Army during World War II.

C20. **Stalin, Joseph.** *Correspondence Between the Chairman of the Council of Ministers of the U.S.S.R. and the Presidents of the U.S.A. and the Prime Ministers of Great Britain During the Great Patriotic War of 1941-1945.* Moscow: Foreign Languages Publishing House, 1957, 2 vols.

This compilation features more material than is found in such titles as *The Secret History of World War II.* Volume I covers correspondence with Churchill and Attlee, whereas Volume II includes Roosevelt and Truman. Some of the Roosevelt and Churchill documents published here appear to have been excluded from *The Secret History.* Editorial annotations would have improved this set; nevertheless, we may still see here some of the truth and some of the Potemkin surface of Stalin as he tried to influence his international colleagues.

C21. Voroshilov, Kliment E. *Stalin and the Armed Forces of the U.S.S.R.* Moscow: Foreign Languages Publishing House, 1951, 151 p.

A propaganda paeon that trumpets the military genius of Stalin, the "greatest man on our planet" (p. 81), as he repeatedly saved and glorified Marxism-Leninism from 1918 through 1951. Voroshilov served as a Politburo member, a Commissar of War, and a Marshal of the Soviet Army, and was a longtime Stalin confidant—although his military reputation is now somewhat mixed.

FOREIGN POLICY

C22. Brandt, Conrad. *Stalin's Failure in China, 1924-1927.* New York: W. W. Norton & Co., 1966, 226 p., bibliography.

Brandt chronicles and comments on the Soviet failure to bring Chinese communism to power in the 1920s. Some think that Brandt ascribes Stalin and Trotsky's lack of success to their supposed over-reliance on proletarian power; however, such idealism would not seem to fit with Stalin's pragmatic and unsentimental ethos. Provides material of interest on early Soviet methods of exporting a revolution, but presumes much knowledge of other research.

C23. Leonhard, Wolfgang. *Betrayal: The Hitler-Stalin Pact of 1939.* New York: St. Martin's Press, 1989, 215 p., bibliography.

The author relates the story of the Soviet-German agreement of 1939, how it somewhat furtively divided Eastern Europe, and how non-Russian communists reacted. Leonhard makes the perhaps atypical case that Stalin actually harmed his own cause by delaying war. Some readers may find this hard to accept, considering Stalin's earlier purge of the Russian officer corps and the resulting need to rebuild the military hierarchy's leadership and organizational structure.

C24. **Ree, Erik van.** *Socialism in One Zone: Stalin's Policy in Korea, 1945-1947.* Oxford: Berg, 1989, 299 p., bibliography.

Ree makes the case for the argument that Stalin did not wish to risk war with the United States in 1945, and therefore eliminated those Korean communists wanting to take over the entire Korean Peninsula. The author shows the Soviet leader as desiring to solidify territorial security won by the Red Army at the close of World War II rather than immediately risking another conflagration. This theory might or might not fit with the developing Berlin crisis, wherein Stalin held on to the surrounding territory but did take a enormous gamble by confronting American military might.

C25. **Shulman, Marshall Darrow.** *Stalin's Foreign Policy Reappraised.* New York: Atheneum, 1963, 320 p., bibliography.

Shulman contends that Stalin himself began to change Soviet foreign policy following the Berlin Blockade, and that he recognized non-belligerent or peaceful coexistence with the West as perhaps necessary to the long-term survival of both countries. The author shows how both domestic affairs and international changes worked to alter Soviet foreign policy. He does not, however, go back much further than 1949, and does not provide as much Asian coverage as might be desired. Nevertheless, this is an excellent study which has stood the test of time.

C26. **Topitsch, Ernst.** *Stalin's War: A Radical New Theory of the Origins of the Second World War.* New York: St. Martin's Press, 1987, 152 p., bibliography.

The author believes that Stalin used the United States, Japan, and Great Britain to fight one another in order to destroy the capitalist world. In general, the book was poorly received and criticized for factual errors and lack of supporting documentation.

C27. Ulam, Adam B. *Expansion and Co-Existence: The History of Soviet Foreign Policy, 1917-1967.* New York: Praeger Publishers, 1968, 775 p.

Ulam portrays Stalinistic foreign policy as arising from the dictator's innate suspicion of the West and other areas, and from a longstanding Russian impulse to push its frontiers outward as a defense against internal decay. Ulam believes Stalin's successors never achieved his level of concentrated power, but that they had to deal with a more complex group of both supporters and opponents.

STALIN AND THE WEST

C28. Baciu, Nicolas. *Sell-out to Stalin: The Tragic Errors of Churchill and Roosevelt: The Untold Story.* New York: Vantage Press, 1984, 299 p., bibliography.

This self-published tabloid effort contends that the Western leaders actually began to cede Eastern Europe to Russia as early as 1941 and that Churchill consciously played the greater role in this giveaway. The case of Rumania receives special attention. F.D.R. is portrayed as something of a sickly dictator, and Churchill as a man also suffering from enough health problems seriously to affect his judgment. Stalin comes across as an aggressive and cunning manipulator.

C29. Columbia University. Russian Institute. *The Anti-Stalin Campaign and International Communism: A Selection of Documents.* Rev. ed. New York: Columbia University Press, 1956, 342 p.

After reprinting a U.S. State Department copy of the closed Khrushchev report of 1956—that perhaps officially began the Soviet denunciation of Stalin—this book presents a compilation of communist-party reactions. These come from the United States, Italy, France, Great Britain, and the U.S.S.R. (from the newspaper, *Pravda*).

C30. **Edmonds, Robin.** *The Big Three: Churchill, Roosevelt, and Stalin in Peace & War.* New York: W. W. Norton & Co., 1991, 608 p., bibliography.

Robins examines the tripartite relationship during the Second World War between the United States, the Soviet Union, and Great Britain, tracing the roots of their relations back to the early 1930s, when Hitler first came to power. The author does not place any of the three Allied leaders in the category of "horizon-breakers" (Preface). Stalin's diplomatic character and experience is examined more fully than his political side, a focus also followed during the War by Roosevelt and Churchill, out of military necessary. Stalin is here given some credit for conceiving the ideals as well as the framework of the United Nations, which credit may or may not conflict with the Soviet leader's tyrannical domestic methods.

C31. **Fischer, Louis.** *The Road to Yalta: Soviet Foreign Relations, 1941-1945.* New York: Harper & Row, 1972, 238 p., bibliography.

The author believes that Stalin took full advantage of Roosevelt's desire for a joint Soviet-American entente, and that Poland's sacrifice really sealed the communist fate for the rest of Eastern Europe. Fischer contends that much of the European reapportionment had been decided before the Yalta Conference. Some critics felt that the book did not make any significant new arguments.

C32. **Gruber, Helmut.** *Soviet Russia Masters the Comintern: International Communism in the Era of Stalin's Ascen-*

dancy. Garden City, NY: Anchor Press, 1974, 544 p., bibliography.

Gruber brings together documents by other hands in an effort to persuade readers that Stalin bent international communism to his will between 1924 and 1931. Some critics do not feel that the materials used actually show such docility on the part of non-Soviet Marxists. This book is a loose sequel to an earlier volume covering the Lenin era.

C33. **Kennan, George F.** *Russia and the West Under Lenin and Stalin.* Boston: Little, Brown & Co., 1961, 411 p.

A group of essays derived from lectures given at Harvard and Oxford, *Russian and the West Under Lenin and Stalin* covers Soviet foreign policy through the Second World War. Kennan argues that the primary diplomatic aim of Lenin and Stalin towards the West was to undermine its existence. The author served as U.S. ambassador to the U.S.S.R.; his considerable insight and wit and experience are evident throughout these highly readable reflections.

C34. **Kusnierz, Bronislaw.** *Stalin and the Poles: An Indictment of the Soviet Leaders.* London: Hollis & Carter, 1949, 317 p.

Kusnierz compares Soviet and German attempts at destroying Polish identity, culture, and political independence, and concludes that Stalin's methods showed greater planning and psychological cunning than those of his Nazi counterparts. The author accuses the Soviets of the Katyn Forest Massacre and many other crimes, and claims that Poland was an early example of what Stalin planned for the world. There are no footnotes or background materials. The writer was a former justice minister in the Polish government of General Bor-Komorowski.

C35. **Laloy, Jean.** *Yalta: Yesterday, Today, Tomorrow.* New York: Harper & Row, 1990, 153 p., bibliography.

The author describes F.D.R.'s last big meeting with his Russian counterpart, and relates how Stalin tried to manipulate the situation for post-war gains. Laloy contrasts the characters of these two leaders, maintaining that Stalin's cunning strategy was maintained in later Soviet chiefs of state to one degree or another. He also argues that the decisions of Yalta set the tone for the ensuing Cold War throughout Europe. Translated from the French original.

C36. **McSherry, James E.** *Stalin, Hitler, and Europe.* Cleveland: World Publishing Co., 1968-70, 2 vols., bibliography.

McSherry argues that Stalin played the Germans off against the Anglo-French alliance to protect himself from Hitler. The Soviet dictator is given credit for his tactical maneuvers, but also receives strategic chiding for giving Germany time to assault the West and to further build its military machine. From a perhaps paranoid viewpoint, Stalin may not have seen much choice but to play his dangerous game as long as possible.

C37. **Miner, Steven M.** *Between Churchill and Stalin: The Soviet Union, Great Britain, and the Origins of the Grand Alliance.* Chapel Hill, NC: University of North Carolina Press, 1988, 319 p., bibliography.

Argues that Stalin's very strong urge to expand Soviet frontiers actually foreshadowed much of the Cold War tension even before the 1941-42 formation of the Grand Alliance. Miner believes that the British demonstrated an unrealistic approach to diplomacy that sharply contrasted with Stalin's hard-headed methods.

C38. **Nadeau, Remi A.** *Stalin, Churchill, and Roosevelt Divide Europe.* New York: Praeger Publishers, 1990, 259 p., bibliography.

Nadeau promotes the idea that Stalin took advantage of Roosevelt's idealism, and that Churchill did not have the military means to prevent the Soviet absorption of Eastern Europe. He traces the main story back to 1941 in trying to show how Churchill's efforts to warn and persuade his American counterpart foundered on Roosevelt's desire to mediate differences and to rely on unenforceable agreements. Some historians believe that the Cold War gained much momentum as a result of the diplomatic campaign herein described.

C39. **Nisbet, Robert A.** *Roosevelt and Stalin: The Failed Courtship.* Washington, DC: Regnery Gateway, 1988, 120 p.

The author makes the case that F.D.R. conceded as much territory and influence as possible to his Soviet counterpart in order to win him over to the cause of global peace and participative government. Nisbet also writes that the American president saw British colonialism as a greater threat to democracy than communism, and that he ignored the cautionary warnings of advisors such as George Kennan and W. Averell Harriman. The 1943 Tehran conference—rather than the later Yalta meeting—is seen as the point of Stalin's diplomatic victory, with Roosevelt echoing a role played in the late 1930s by Neville Chamberlain.

C40. **O'Neill, William L.** *A Better World: Stalinism and the American Intellectuals.* New Brunswick, NJ: Transaction Publishers, 1990, 447 p., bibliography.

O'Neill's work studies the effect of Stalin's policies and Stalinism on American intellectuals' views of the relationship between the United States and the Soviet Union from 1939 to the mid-1950s. The intellectuals were non-communists, but were still liberal enough to have a generally sympathetic view of the Soviet Union and its aspirations. Originally published in 1982.

C41. **Read, Anthony, and David Fisher.** *The Deadly Embrace: Hitler, Stalin, and the Nazi-Soviet Pact, 1939-1941.* New York: W. W. Norton & Co., 1988, 687 p., bibliography.

A dramatically readable account of the infamous Russo-German liaison period. Drawn largely from secondary publications and English-language materials, *The Deadly Embrace* does not reveal startling new information but concentrates on giving an interesting, in-depth look at the events and the leaders. The authors allege that the Russian dictator had to persuade the populace of his leadership value in order to remain in power, which might prove true to the extent that any tyrant must blend a certain amount of deception with a great deal of raw coercive power.

C42. **Richardson, Stewart, ed.** *The Secret History of World War II: The Ultra-Secret Wartime Letters and Cables of Roosevelt, Stalin and Churchill.* New York: Richardson and Steirman, 1987, 277 p.

The selection here does not include some items found in the 1957 two-volume edition published by the Soviet Ministry of Foreign Affairs (*Correspondence Between the Chairman...* [item C20]). The latter adds documents involving Attlee and Truman along with additional pieces to or from Roosevelt and Churchill. Unfortunately, Richardson fails to provide commentary or other supplemental information on the archival sources for these documents. Still, the materials reveal something of the Soviet leader's character as he tried to play off his Allied colleagues against one another.

C43. Rieber, Alfred J. *Stalin and the French Communist Party, 1941-1947.* New York: Columbia University Press, 1962, 395 p., bibliography.

Rieber recounts the story of how Stalin's government thoroughly controlled and misguided the French communists both during the Resistance and after the Liberation. As with some other works in this bibliography, much of the text is based on external, non-Soviet documents. Some critics felt that the book did not sufficiently explain Stalin's manipulative methods.

C44. Roberts, Geoffrey K. *The Unholy Alliance: Stalin's Pact with Hitler.* Bloomington: Indiana University Press, 1989, 296 p., bibliography.

The author concentrates on the Soviet side of the story in showing how Stalin deceptively planned the 1939 agreement with Hitler in order to buy time for Russia's weakened military establishment (whose leadership had been decimated by Stalin's recent purges). Roberts uses established materials, the text of the German-Russian friendship treaty, and some newly revealed, mostly secondary sources to contend that the original agreement did not specifically carve up Poland as later determined by secret protocol. Also supported is the argument that the entente did not entirely remove a certain vagueness from Stalin's foreign policy.

C45. Rosenberg, William, ed. *Social and Cultural History of the Soviet Union: The Lenin and Stalin Years.* New York: Garland Publishing Co., 1992, 519 p.

This anthology of articles by many different scholars presents materials on several important issues: "the socio-economic basis for early Bolshevik power, the rise of the Stalin personality cult, the social background to collectivization, the formation of new Soviet elites, World War II and the origins of the Cold War, and the importance of the Khrushchev years as a point of transition to perestroika"—Publisher's note. Materials are organized into three sections: "The Early Years: Peasants, Workers, Traders," "Culture, Ideology, Technology," and "Gender and Family." A valuable collection to provide a broad overview of its subject.

C46. **Sainsbury, Keith.** *The Turning Point: Roosevelt, Stalin, Churchill, and Chiang Kai-Shek, 1943: The Moscow, Cairo, and Tehran Conferences.* Oxford: Oxford University Press, 1985, 373 p., bibliography.

The author examines the series of wartime meetings between the three major allied leaders as high-level bargaining sessions that dealt with real disagreements. Tehran receives the greatest attention. Stalin's interests would seem to have benefitted from the picture here of F.D.R. as a politician who tried to rationalize differences with the Soviet leader, and who openly criticized Churchill in order to curry Soviet favor.

C47. **Spriano, Paolo.** *Stalin and the European Communists.* London: Verso, 1985, 315 p., bibliography.

Spriano summarizes the European communist experience between 1935 and 1948, when the Cominform took over from the Comintern. Except in countries such as France and Czechoslovakia, where communists had served in coalition governments, each of the parties underwent purges similar to those which occurred in the motherland during the late 1930s. The author censures Stalin rather than anyone else for these violent excesses, and for other organizational problems which plagued the European communist parties.

C48. **Steininger, Rolf.** *The German Question: The Stalin Note of 1952 and the Problem of Reunification.* New York: Columbia University Press, 1990, 186 p., bibliography.

The author argues that Stalin's negotiation efforts on German reunification should have received greater support in the West, and suggests that West German Chancellor Conrad Adenauer persuaded Britain and the United States to leave the negotiations due to his fear that the Germans might well vote to reunite regardless of the conditions imposed by the Soviets (*e.g.*, an agreement not to enter a coalition against any of the German enemies of World War II). Steininger also contends that Stalin made his offer from credible motives, such as encouraging internal Western conflict by building up Germany and Japan, and pursuing the broad policy of peaceful coexistence. Translated from the 1985 German edition.

C49. Taubman, William. *Stalin's American Policy: From Entente to Detente to Cold War.* New York: W. W. Norton & Co., 1982, 291 p., bibliography.

Taubman describes the period from 1941-1953 as one in which Stalin moved the Soviet Union from an initial measure of agreement with the West toward eventual disagreement and Cold War suspicion, and finally worse. The dictator comes across as rather distrustful of the U.S. from the start, and perhaps as unwilling to descend from detente without Western provocation. At the same time, Taubman argues that Stalin was quite willing to erode the post-war strength of the U.S., Great Britain, and their allies, while not completely breaking relations.

C50. Taylor, Sally J. *Stalin's Apologist: Walter Duranty, the New York Times's Man in Moscow.* New York: Oxford University Press, 1990, 404 p., bibliography.

The focus of this book is newspaperman Walter Duranty, whose views on Stalin and events in the Soviet Union in the 1920s and '30s played such an important role in shaping American opinion. Taylor provides solid material regarding Duranty's feelings about Stalin, and discusses the newspaperman's style of reporting. The 1932-1933 Ukrainian famine, largely ignored by many reporters, receives some emphasis. Duranty early predicted

Stalin's rise to power and later accepted the purge trials at face value.

STALIN AND TITO

C51. **Armstrong, Hamilton Fish.** *Tito and Goliath.* New York: Macmillan Publishing Co., 1951, 312 p.

A contemporary account of Tito's break with Stalin, written by an editor of *Foreign Affairs* and former U.S. diplomat who suggested continuing American aid to Yugoslavia. In this early Cold War treatise, Armstrong does not romanticize Tito but does demonstrate the kind of *realpolitik* bartering brought about by the West's great fear of Stalin.

C52. **Banac, Ivo.** *With Stalin Against Tito: Cominformist Splits in Yugoslav Communism.* Ithaca, NY: Cornell University Press, 1988, 294 p., bibliography.

Banac recounts the 1948 Cominform declaration that ejected Yugoslavia from the Eastern European bloc. Stalin motivated the action, and Banac posits that Tito reacted by greatly mistreating the Balkan Stalinists. An important source book covering a personal and a political schism, one that draws upon materials from the Hoover Institution, and from numerous memoirs and journals of the time.

C53. **Dedijer, Vladimir.** *The Battle Stalin Lost: Memoirs of Yugoslavia, 1948-1953.* New York: Viking, 1971, 341 p.

Dedijer's book is a series of personal reminiscences rather than a scholarly treatise, describing how Stalin and Tito struggled for the ultimate control of Yugoslavia. Dedijer greatly admired the Yugoslavian leader and writes of Stalin's efforts as a betrayal of true bolshevism.

The author also takes time to attack the reactionary powers of the United States.

C54. **Dedijer, Vladimir.** *Tito Speaks: His Self Portrait and Struggle with Stalin.* London: Weidenfeld and Nicolson, 1953, 456 p.

The author mixes long passages by Tito with commentary by himself into a book which is simultaneously reminiscence and biography, including an extensive section on Stalin and his efforts to dominate Yugoslavia. Dedijer presents his undocumented work with the view that Tito was "the conscience that Stalin had lost"—Preface.

C55. **Djilas, Milovan.** *Conversations with Stalin.* New York: Harcourt, Brace & World, 1962, 211 p.

Conversations with Stalin describes the author's experiences with the Soviet tyrant during his 1944-1948 visits to Russia as a Yugoslav official. He also speaks of the great disillusionment felt when Stalin tried to undermine Yugoslav nationalism. A number of reviewers commented on the unremarkable writing style of Djilas, and the book received quite varied evaluations as to its credibility and worth.

THE DOCTOR'S PLOT

C56. **Rapoport, Louis.** *Stalin's War Against the Jews: The Doctor's Plot and the Soviet Solution.* New York: Free Press, 1990, 318 p., bibliography.

Rapoport studies the development of Stalin's anti-Semitism from his seminary training to the Jew-hatred of his adopted country, Russia. These feelings played a role in his later persecution of Trotsky and the other Jewish Bolsheviks who had played such a large role in the October Revolution. A major portion of this book is devoted to the Doctor's Plot of 1953, when a group of Jewish physicians was accused of killing or planning to kill Soviet government officials. Only Stalin's death stopped what was possibly the beginning of a major anti-Semitic campaign. The author based much of his work on newly released archival materials and personal interviews. Many quotes from Stalin's speeches and conversations demonstrate the depths of his anti-Semitism.

C57. **Rapoport, Yakov.** *The Doctor's Plot of 1953.* Cambridge, MA: Harvard University Press, 1991, 280 p.

These memoirs, written by a pathologist who was accused of planning to kill important Soviet leaders, give the reader a valuable and personal insight into the terror of Stalin's last year. The government-inspired lawlessness and anti-Semitism of the early 1950s is described in a most personal manner, since it actually happened to the author. The Doctor's Plot of 1953 is considered the first step in Stalin's last full-scale terror campaign—the prelude to a major anti-Semitic pogrom. The government campaign was quietly dropped and the prisoners released shortly after Stalin's death. An introduction by Rapoport's daughter relates the effect her father's arrest had on her and her family, and their attempt to survive under extremely difficult circumstances.

D.

FICTION AND JUVENILE NONFICTION

FICTION AND DRAMA ABOUT STALIN

D1. **De, Oleksander.** *Stalin: Persona Non Grata: A Verse Play in Three Acts.* London: Mitre Press, 1969, 102 p.

The dictator comes across as paranoid, haunted, yet seemingly unrepentant in this brief drama. Historical and other characters featured include: Kirov, Molotov, Allilujeva, Kalinin, Budu, Koganovich, George, Elena, Beria, Svetlana, and the Madman.

D2. **Grossman, Vasilii Semenovich.** *Life and Fate: A Novel.* New York: Harper & Row, 1986, 880 p.

Concerned with the Great Patriotic War (World War II) and its effect on Russia, this lengthy novel is included in this bibliography because of its materials critical of Stalin, its insights into Stalinist society, and the author's emphasis on the importance of the individual. Grossman's earlier novel, *Forever Flowing* (New York: Harper & Row, 1972), also includes material on the Stalin era, but with a greater emphasis on Lenin. Indirectly, Grossman attacks the Cult of Personality and questions Stalin's military leadership.

D3. **Jones, Mervyn.** *Joseph.* New York: Atheneum, 1970, 506 p.

A fictionalized biography that offers enough personalization and psychological insight to satisfy some but not all the critics. May not fully cover the manipulative traits of Stalin deduced or described by many scholars and observers.

D4. **Koestler, Arthur.** *Darkness at Noon.* New York: Macmillan Publishing Co., 1941, 267 p.

Koestler's fictional account of Soviet history and the Moscow trials of 1936 and 1937 is now considered a classic of anti-Soviet and anti-Stalin literature. Based in part on the author's personal experience, the novel gives the reader a feeling of life in a police state. The book relates the story of an old revolutionary (perhaps Bukharin or Trotsky) who is killed by Stalin.

D5. **Krotkov, Yuri.** *The Red Monarch: Scenes from the Life of Stalin.* New York: W. W. Norton & Co., 1979, 253 p.

Krotkov's fictionalized biography of Stalin creatively combines historical and imaginary events. While humanizing Stalin, the author manages to capture the ruler's power and personality without excusing his actions. Since it is difficult to tell fact from fiction, the reader needs to exercise caution. The reviews were mixed but generally positive.

D6. **Orwell, George.** *Animal Farm.* New York: Harcourt, Brace and Co., 1946, 118 p.

This satire on dictatorship is an allegory of Stalin's rise to power and his methods of rule. A group of farm animals overthrow a cruel master and establish a utopia which quickly deteriorates into a dictatorship. A classic novel and highly recommended.

D7. **Orwell, George.** *Nineteen Eighty-Four.* New York: Harcourt, Brace, 1949, 314 p.

Orwell's classic story of a collectivist society in which the government controls all aspects of life is considered a bitter satire on Communist Russia under Stalin as well as a chilling science-fiction portrait of what might happen elsewhere. Orwell portrays the supposedly future government in terms of a sociological and psychological nightmare wherein the truth and the individual are both abused and distorted. Although Stalin is never mentioned, the description of the "leader" clearly leaves the reader with the impression that Orwell is using Stalin as a model.

D8. **Rybakov, Anatolii.** *Children of the Arbat.* Boston: Little, Brown & Co., 1988, 685 p.

The Arbat, a famous district in the heart of Moscow, is home to the main characters of this novel. In a partly autobiographical manner, Rybakov portrays a picture of Soviet society in the early years of Stalin's rule up to Kirov's murder in 1934. Stalin is an important character in the novel, and, although not the central character, certainly the dominant one. This is one of the best fictionalizations of Stalin by a Soviet writer, and received excellent reviews on publication. This is the first part of a projected three-volume "Arbat Trilogy," the second volume of which, *Fear*, was published in late 1992.

D9. **Shalamov, Varlam Tikhonovich.** *Graphite.* New York: W. W. Norton & Co., 1981, 287 p.

Like the author's *Kolyma Tales* [item D10], this title provides more dark examples of how Siberian exiles were physically crushed and spiritually dehumanized by the Stalinist machine. Shalamov wrote his horror stories from the perspective of one who had survived many years in prison camps and who overcame the instinct to forget the entire nightmare.

D10. **Shalamov, Varlam Tikhonovich.** *Kolyma Tales.* New York: W. W. Norton & Co., 1980, 222 p.

This group of short stories brings to grim life the very painful experiences and gray-to-black emotions of the millions of Gulag victims in northeast Siberia. Shalamov's artistic description symbolizes what happened to the internal émigrés of the Stalinist Police system, as based upon the author's own experience of seventeen years as a prisoner in the Kolyma region.

D11. **Sholokhov, Mikhail.** *Virgin Soil Up-Turned.* Harmondsworth, England: Penguin Books, 1977, 375 p.

Sholokhov's novel tells the story of the forced collectivization and the liquidation of the kulaks in one Cossack area of the U.S.S.R. as a result of Stalin's modernization policies begun in the late 1920s. Although Sholokhov actually received Soviet approval of this and other works, he still was able to artistically convey—perhaps in spite of himself—some of the peasant tragedy as well as the bureaucratic absurdity of the situation. The Nobel-prize-winning author gained less English-language acclaim for this book than for his *And Quiet Flows the Don*, as certain reviewers felt *Virgin Soil* fell short of his other work in characterization and sweep. The first American edition of 1935 carried the title, *Seeds of Tomorrow*.

D12. **Solzhenitsyn, Aleksandr.** *The First Circle.* New York: Harper & Row, 1968, 580 p.

In part autobiographical, this novel describes life in a scientific research institute during four days in 1949. The institute is in fact a penal colony for political prisoners. Through conversations and images Stalin is placed at the center of the story. In one of the most important novels devoted to the Soviet leader, *The First Circle* examines Stalin and his dictatorship at length. A detailed analysis of the novel can be found in Rosalind Marsh's book, *Images of Dictatorship: Portraits of Stalin in Literature* [item B93].

D. FICTION AND JUVENILE NONFICTION

D13. **Solzhenitsyn, Aleksandr.** *One Day in the Life of Ivan Denisovich.* New York: Praeger Publishers, 1963, 210 p.

One of the most popular and important works of fiction written about life under Stalin, *One Day* simply relates the story of twenty-four hours in the life of a typical prisoner in one of Stalin's labor camps. The descriptions of camp life and the struggle to survive are vividly and realistically presented—and the shadow of Stalin is always present. An earlier version was published in 1958.

D14. **Zinoviev, Aleksandr.** *The Yawning Heights.* New York: Random House, 1979, 828 p.

A scathing satire on the Soviet system including the Stalin era. Stalin, called "The Boss," is subject to satiric derision, as is his cult and the society he helped create. Although the book received mixed reviews, it is valuable as a biting literary examination of the dictator and his philosophy.

JUVENILE NONFICTION

D15. **Archer, Jules.** *Man of Steel: Joseph Stalin.* Folkestone, Kent: Bailey Brothers and Swinfen, 1974, 191 p., bibliography.

Intended for young adults, this reprint of a 1965 biography committed some factual mistakes, yet still received some critical praise for its neutral presentation. Provides a useful background on Russian history and on communism.

D16. **Blassingame, Wyatt.** *Joseph Stalin and Communist Russia.* Champaign, IL: Garrard Publishing Co., 1971, 175 p.

107

Blassingame covers Stalin's entire life and includes parts of his speeches as well as words from those who met or worked with him. Also features a chronology and glossary. May be easier to follow than Archer's *Man of Steel*... [item D15], and therefore a better choice for grades 5-7.

D17. **Caulkins, Janet.** *Joseph Stalin.* New York: Franklin Watts, 1991, 160 p., bibliography.

The author provides a thorough overview of Stalin's life and times, and introduces juvenile readers (grades 7-12) to the different sides of this dynamic and perhaps puzzling leader. Caulkins portrays the dictator as a brutal and crazed politician, as a driven administrator who transformed the U.S.S.R. into an industrial powerhouse, and as a steadfast military ruler.

D18. **Gibson, Michael.** *Russia Under Stalin.* New York: G. P. Putnam's Sons, 1972, 128 p., bibliography.

Gibson describes Stalin's development against the backdrop of Czarist Russia, and then relates how the dictator gained power and remained in control from the purges of the 1930s through the Second World War and after. Includes a chronology of major events from 1879-1961. Suggested for grades 7-12.

D19. **Hayes, David, and F. H. Gregory.** *Joseph Stalin.* Hove, England: Wayland, 1977, 96 p.

This secondary school text attempts to provide an objective picture of Stalin while acknowledging the unusual absence of substantiated sources.

D20. **Hoobler, Dorothy, and Thomas Hoobler.** *Joseph Stalin.* New York: Chelsea House, 1985, 112 p., bibliography.

A work perhaps best used by grades 6-9, this book credits Stalin with considerable industrialization and military strengthening of the Soviet Union, but also holds him responsible for the systematic brutal dehumanization that cost millions of lives. The Hooblers do not evade such matters as the alleged suicide of Stalin's wife or his possible arrangement of Trotsky's murder. Liberally illustrated with black-and-white photos and drawings.

D21. **Jacobs, William Jay.** *Stalin.* Beverly Hills, CA: Benziger, 1976, 95 p., bibliography.

A brief biography suitable for junior high school students or anyone older wishing a quick overview, *Stalin* is illustrated with numerous black-and-white photos. Stalin is portrayed as a great leader who used evil methods to build the Soviet Union into a world power.

D22. **Liversidge, Douglas.** *Joseph Stalin.* New York: Franklin Watts, 1969, 188 p.

Liversidge follows a companion volume on Lenin with this new book, which claims that Stalin took advantage of errors by his more idealistic predecessor to greatly expand his own personal hegemony. The author describes how a harsh childhood may explain some of the dictator's crueller traits. Also covers Stalin's industrialization efforts and his role in the Second World War. Includes a chronology and photographs. *Joseph Stalin* is perhaps best suited for grades 6-8.

D23. **Marrin, Albert.** *Stalin.* New York: Viking Kestrel, 1988, 244 p., bibliography.

One of the best biographies of Stalin written for the younger reader, Marrin's book focuses on the dictator, while simultaneously providing a good deal of background material on pre-revolutionary Czarist Russia and on the Russian Revolution of 1917. Throughout the book the author shows the influence of Stalin on all aspects of

Soviet history and how the power of one man can influence history. An excellent introductory work, best suited for grades 7 and higher.

D24. **McCauley, Martin.** *The Stalin File.* London: Batsford, 1979, 96 p., bibliography.

McCauley's fairly negative view of Stalin includes many quotes, both from the ruler himself and from those around him. The author mentions such points as Lenin's disillusionment with Stalin, the mass suffering brought by collectivization, the brutal illegality of the purges, and Stalin's apparently stumbling diffidence during the opening battles with Germany. The book closes with a chronology, a list of Stalin's pseudonyms, a brief biographical section on his Soviet contemporaries, a glossary of terms and organizations, and bibliographies of related books and audiovisual sources. Heavily illustrated with black-and-white photographs, tables, and other materials, *The Stalin File* is best suited for grades 7-10.

D25. **Paley, Alan L.** *Stalin: The Iron-Fisted Dictator of Russia.* Charlotteville, NY: Sam Har Press, 1971, 32 p., bibliography.

Paley describes Stalin as one of the most despised men of the Twentieth Century, but contends that he did not consciously pursue evil the way Hitler did. Rather, the author asserts that the Soviet ruler displayed a consistently milder disposition than his German counterpart. Regarding the Great Purge, Paley argues that Hitler may have leaked knowledge of possible Russian military plots against the dictator to induce Stalin's decision to slaughter many of the top Soviet generals.

D26. **Stacey, Francis William, ed.** *Stalin and the Making of Modern Russia.* London: Edward Arnold, 1970, 64 p., bibliography.

Seventy extracts from newspapers, interviews, speeches, novels, treaties, autobiographies, and other sources cover Stalin's entire life, and range from the flattering to the bitter to the propagandistic. Included are items by Lenin, Trotsky, Sidney and Beatrice Webb, Winston Churchill, Andrei Vyshinsky, Boris Pasternak, and—most frequently—Stalin himself. The editor cautions his readers in the introduction to be wary of source documents. He begins each chapter with background notes and closes each one with a list of classroom-type questions.

D27. *Stalin: Pro & Con.* New York: Columbia House, 1977, 160 p., bibliography.

A helpful split format in this anthology places an overall biographical summary at the top of each page, with excerpted and sometimes variant accounts of important events taking up two columns on the lower part. Thus, in the chapter on domestic policies and purges, we find among the various sub-sections: comments on the kolkhoz by Trotsky, a piece by De Gaulle on Stalin's czar-like status, and a bit of speculation from *Life* magazine and elsewhere on the murder of Sergei Kirov. Interspersed throughout are expressive, photo-like illustrations in black-and-white. This work could serve as an excellent, abridged overview for readers of any age, as well as an assignment source for students in grades 7-12. Translated from the original 1971 Italian edition.

AUTHOR INDEX

Lampert, Nicholas, B22
Laqueur, Walter, A47, B23
Leonhard, Wolfgang, C23
Levine, Isaac Don, A14, A48
Levytsky, Borys, C11
Lewin, Moshe, A49, B82, C2
Lewis, Jonathan, A50
Lipkov, Alexander, B84
Litvinov, Maxim, A51
Liversidge, Douglas, D22
Ludwig, Emil, A16
Lynch, Michael, B24
Lyons, Eugene, A17, B25
Maisky, Ivan, A52
Mandel'shtam, Nadezhda, B83
Marrin, Albert, D23
Marsh, Rosalind J., B93, B94
Marx-Engels-Lenin Institute, A18
Matlock, Jack F., A80
McCagg, William O., B59
McCauley, Martin, A53, D24
McNeal, Robert Hatch, A54, A81, B26, B60
McSherry, James E., C36
Medvedev Brothers—SEE: Khrushchev, Nikita S., and Medvedev, Roy Aleksandrovich, and Medvedev, Zhores Aleksandrovich
Medvedev, Roy Aleksandrovich, A55, B19, B27, B28
Medvedev, Zhores Aleksandrovich, B19, B99
Mehnert, Klaus, B61
Merridale, Catherine, B62
Mikhailkov-Konchalovskii, Andrei Sergeevich, B84
Miller, Frank J., B85
Miner, Steven M., C37
Molotov, V. M., *et al.*, A19
Murphy, John Thomas. A20
Nadeau, Remi A., C38
Nekrich, Aleksandr, B17
Nicolaevsky, Boris I., A56, B19
Nisbet, Robert A., C39
Nove, Alec, B29, B73, B86

117

TITLE INDEX

Stalin's Prosecutor, C14
Stalin's Russia, B21
Stalin's Russia: An Historical Reconsideration, B32
Stalin's Russia and the Crisis in Socialism, A9
Stalin's Secret War, B39
Stalin's Special Departments, B65
Stalin's War, C26
Stalin's War Against the Jews, C56
Stalin's Works, A81
Svetlana: The Story of Stalin's Daughter, A34
Technology and Society Under Lenin and Stalin, B97
Testimony, A62
The Three Dictators, A21
Three Who Made a Revolution, A72
The Time of Stalin, A28
Tito and Goliath, C51
Tito Speaks, C54
Total Revolution, B8
Totalitarian Art, B91
Trotsky, Stalin, and Socialism, B13
The Truth About Stalin, B19
The Tukhachevsky Affair, C15
The Turning Point, C46
Twenty Letters to a Friend, A27
The Unholy Alliance, C44
Utopia in Power, B17
Virgin Soil Upturned, D11
The War, 1941-1945, A35
Why Lenin? Why Stalin? A Reappraisal of the Russian Revolution, 1900-1930, B46
With Stalin Against Tito, C52
With Stalin: Memoirs, A42
Within the Whirlwind, A36
Witness to History, 1929-1969, A6
The Wolf of the Kremlin, A45
Works [Stalin], A87
Yalta: Yesterday, Today, Tomorrow, C35
The Yawning Heights, D14
Years Off My Life, A37
The Young Stalin, A64

ABOUT THE AUTHORS

MARTY BLOOMBERG is Head of Collection Development at the John M. Pfau Library, California State University, San Bernardino. Since joining CSUSB in 1966, he has worked in several administrative as well as faculty positions within the library, including Associate Director of the Library.

Bloomberg is the author of six books, several of which have gone through multiple editions, including two standard library science texts: *Introduction to Technical Services for Library Technicians* and *Introduction to Public Services for Library Technicians.* He has also compiled two other bibliographies, *World War II and Its Origins* (with Hans Weber), and *The Jewish Holocaust: An Annotated Guide to Books in English* (Borgo, 1991).

He is married, has two children, and lives with his wife, Leila, an elementary school principal, in Riverside, California.

BUCKLEY BARRY BARRETT has been head of Technical Services at the John M. Pfau Library, California State University, San Bernardino, since 1987. Barrett joined the faculty of CSUSB in 1982, and has worked in various reference and cataloging assignments. He was the manager of the KeyNotis Automated System Project from 1989-1991.

He has also written *The Barstow Printer: A Personal Name and Subject Index to the Years 1910-1920* (Borgo, 1985). He has completed two other books—*World War I: A Cataloging Reference Guide* and *World War II: A Cataloging Reference Guide*—and is working on another, a second edition of *The Jewish Holocaust: An Annotated Guide to Books in English* (with Marty Bloomberg), all for The Borgo Press.

He is married, has two children, and lives with his wife, Nannette (also a librarian), in San Bernardino, California.

www.ingramcontent.com/pod-product-compliance
Lightning Source LLC
LaVergne TN
LVHW091153080426
835509LV00006B/661